At Home
Ten Years Collecting
From Historic
Scotland

Text by
Hugh Cheape, George Dalgleish, Elizabeth Wright and Jane Kidd

Photographs by
Ian Larner and Doreen Moyes

NATIONAL MUSEUM
OF ANTIQUITIES OF SCOTLAND

EDINBURGH
HER MAJESTY'S STATIONERY OFFICE

ISBN 0 11 492384 1

Contents

At Home

The National Museum of Antiquities of Scotland has had a long and distinguished career over two hundred years. It was created as the collection of the Society of Antiquaries of Scotland, itself the great and lasting achievement of one of Scotland's patriots, David Erskine, Earl of Buchan. This energetic and quixotic nobleman was the beau idéal of the noble patron, who unlike many a noble patron bore uncomplainingly the responsibilities and self-sacrifice which this venture entailed. He was determined to provide Scotland with the most effective means of safeguarding its national heritage and of reinforcing its sense of a national identity. The Society of Antiquaries was founded in 1780, and property and a home for a rapidly growing collection was found in 1781, Buchan himself bearing most of the cost. The Museum's collections have continued to grow by leaps and bounds since then, and have outgrown several homes, a fact as true a hundred years ago as it is today.

Ten years is not a long time in the life span of the National Museum but it is a long time in the experience of those running the Museum at first hand, and in the present framework of public attitude which is always slow to develop or change. The collections have continued to grow by donation and purchase and new areas of Scotland's material culture have been investigated. This is not necessarily because we know more than our predecessors, a conceit that can only sometimes be justified. It is more often because of varying perspectives due to changes in fashion and academic interests. It is not a part of the Museum's role to be swayed by the vagaries of fashion, indeed the Museum can and often does predetermine fashion. But in the wake of fashion and popular attention come sensation and high prices, and the vulgar spectacle of Scotland's national treasure traded to foreign buyers through the auction rooms. This account

shows that, given adverse circumstances, treasures can be and have been accumulated for Scotland. The material illustrated and described belongs to a period from the 17th century to the present day and has all been acquired during the last ten years. It demonstrates what a relatively small national museum has succeeded in doing for its nation when fine art has become big business and such a high price has come to be placed on antiquity.

It would be wrong to suggest that adversity resulted solely from a national museum's unsteady progress in a world of rapidly advancing auction room records, rapidly developing junk culture and the rapidly approaching prospect of mankind's oblivion. Adversity is much more mundane. In the last thirty or forty years, the needs of the Museum for accommodation and staff have been given careful and timely consideration by successive governments, endorsed by a Scottish public which sets great store by a 'national museum'. Official encouragement of the Museum as a valuable educational resource and service was slow in growing and it has been up to the Museum itself to set the pace. The planning for a new Museum on a central site was formally sanctioned in 1952. The project began in earnest in 1964 and took shape over the ensuing decade, absorbing much of the energies of our small staff. The building of a new National Museum was poised to begin when the whole project was postponed in 1976.

This was not of course the end of the National Museum itself, then approaching its two hundredth birthday, although after twenty years of active planning, the decision to postpone was bound to be a demoralising setback. The aims and objectives of the National Museum have not been affected and it has carried on with as much if not more zeal as before. Even if a new building on a new site were the zenith of our ambitions, and even if these ambitions could never be realised all at once, the day-to-day work continues as before and progress is achieved. The ambitions of the future may be different, but at the very least future generations should expect to inherit a well organised national collection. Display space is as ever at a premium and only a small proportion of the national collections can be exhibited at once, but scarce resources can still be allocated to building up a treasure house for Scotland. The treasures which we store up for the future and the treasures which we display are of the highest quality and rank with the best national collections in Europe.

The National Museum has always collected and stored up treasure and our treasure is not just precious metal; it is not just the rare or even the curious or the ancient. In fact, many items of what we might now regard as the treasures of antiquity were not even made when the Museum was founded. This applies particularly to the acquisitions of the last decade or so. From the earliest days of the Museum, 'Antiquities' was interpreted in its widest sense. The larger proportion of the collections was prehistoric but the modern, that is the material culture of the 18th and 19th centuries, was also collected. It was collected for the insight it gave into the ways of societies dead and gone, and it was collected because, even then, there was a strong feeling prevalent that times were changing and the familiar would soon be an irretrievable thing of the past.

Throughout our history variety has been the key to the Museum's acquisitions which originally included foreign ethnological objects, curiosities such as an unusually shaped branch of Scots fir, and natural history specimens like the 16ft long jawbone of a whale. This last was set up as an arch in the grounds of the Museum's first home, a 'large and commodious' house between the east end of St Giles and the Cowgate, and seems to have been the forerunner of many such whalebone arches still to be seen throughout Scotland. One remarkable feature of a museum with such a long history is the high survival rate of the earliest donations. Indeed, it would be a betrayal of our claim to be a museum if we lost things. But one or two donations do seem to have gone missing, perhaps in this case even to our

relief. The 'scalp of a French soldier . . . the queue tied with a pink ribbon' and 'a hand-grenade, charged' were no doubt popular exhibits during the Napoleonic Wars but they have since disappeared. Otherwise, a considerable amount of our exhibits have been transferred to more suitable homes in attempts to rationalise the collections. The Egyptian collection, including two mummies, was given to the Royal Scottish Museum, and at a later date the balance of the non-European comparative collection was also given to our sister institution. Nearly 700 flint implements were transferred to the British Museum. The natural history collections, which gradually came to be outside the National Museum's province as the collections of man-made artifacts grew, were moved to the care of the Royal Society. The Museum has been consistently generous in the provision it has made to other, often younger, institutions.

The early years of the Museum were characterised by dismal fluctuations in its fortunes, and it was forced to change premises four times in its first thirty years of existence. This was in part due to chronic financial difficulties caused by members of the Society failing to pay their subscriptions and creditors pressing for payment; incredible though it may seem, the Museum could not pay the rent for its premises. It can be reassuring to think that our predecessors also had trouble making ends meet. Another problem facing the Museum was evidently the security of the collections, housed as they were in the densely crowded area of Edinburgh, traditionally the haunt of burglars and the demi-monde. Security is still a dilemma which confronts us today, and we always try to achieve a workable balance between ensuring easy access and availability of the objects to the public, and catering for the paramount need to preserve them for future generations. Thankfully, we have not yet had to implement the proposal by the Society's Council in 1785 that as there 'was no defensive weapon in the museum, to be used in the case of an attempt on it by Housebreakers . . . a blunderbuss and large pistols' be purchased for the caretaker.

After doubts over the continuing existence of the Museum or even the likelihood of its survival, it began to revive in the prevailing atmosphere of public interest. This was due to two factors. In the first place, a curiosity about the cultural mysteries of 'North Britain' was sparked off by the works of Ossian and fanned to a flame by Sir Walter Scott whose ballads, narrative poems and novels set the tone of Romanticism in Britain. Secondly and more seriously, there was a new attitude towards antiquities as material evidence capable of supplementing other forms of literary and historical evidence, rather than as curiosities merely to be displayed as such in a showcase. It may have been at this time that enthusiasm for oddities such as the French soldier's scalp faded.

The development of more systematic and scientific methods was helped on by contemporary events, unrelated but of enormous consequence. Agricultural improvement, that process which transformed the face of Scotland between the late 18th century and the early 19th, was bound to throw up evidence of the early acitivity of man. The Museum benefitted from a steady trickle of donations of prehistoric material turned up by the plough and spade. Similar finds are still made today as ploughing continues to go deeper. Field drainage, which spread over all lowland Scotland in the generations after the experiments of James Smith of Deanston in the 1820s, also produced a rich haul of prehistoric finds. The Caledonian Canal, the great white hope for the development of the Highlands, yielded from its foundations in 1808 the first and largest of the massive and impressive Pictish silver chains. This piece came to the Museum as Treasure Trove in 1838. The most critical new source of prehistoric material is strangely reminiscent of the results of speculative development today. The railway mania of the 1840s cut swathes through prehistoric as well as historic sites. Nothing was sacred. Without respite for example, the 15th century Trinity College was demolished in 1848 to make way for the North British Railway Company's Waverley Station in spite of the protests of the Society of Antiquaries.

It may be difficult to imagine a national museum as anything except a very stable and static institution, but mobility was the unhappy keynote of the life of the Society's Museum. After the succession of moves during its first half century, the Museum was included in the new Institution for the Encouragement of the Fine Arts, later the 'Royal Institution', W H Playfair's fine classical building at the foot of the Mound. This ushered in a period of relative prosperity.

At the inaugural meeting in 1826 in the Museum's elegant rooms in the building later to become the Royal Scottish Academy, the Curator gave a report which outlined the aims of the Museum and a philosophy that is still central to our activities today: 'while the accumulation of these relics [of our common ancestors] affords the most likely means of eliciting light upon their general origin, it becomes at the same time the means of converting what is otherwise useless lumber into valuable records of ancient history'. The last phrase is particularly relevant at present, as we are concerned to illustrate the social history of Everyman in our country, and what some people consider 'useless lumber' often turns out to be the very building blocks of history. In this way we have always sought to give the widest possible definition to the concept of national historical and archaeological treasures. Those objects which tell us about the everyday lives of ordinary people are as important to the Museum as the finest artistic treasures created for the rich and powerful. Auntie Jeannie's china chamber-pot can be as interesting in historical terms as the Earl of Hopetoun's silver ewer and basin. All such objects contribute in varying degrees to the rich and colourful tapestry that is Scotland's history. It is the Museum's task to place them in a historical context.

The superficial account of Scotland's past will regurgitate those hoary and well-worn milestones of the short careers of the much-loved Mary Queen of Scots and Bonnie Prince Charlie. They have certainly left us with telling relics, such as the mass of minor articles of clothing and locks of hair shed by Princes Charles Edward while on the run in the Highlands in 1746. As the romantic appeal of Jacobitism grew, these multiplied like fragments of the True Cross. What was recovered from the tragic field of Culloden would fill a warehouse. This reflects our regard for the selfless heroism of those who joined the Jacobite cause, but what else shaped the lives of our forefathers in 1746 and during the two hundred years between Queen Mary and Prince Charles? Here lie the uncharted miles of Scottish society and its material culture, the everyday life not only of the *thrie Estaitis* but also of the *puir pepil,* the *laboraris* of the *grund.*

Towards the middle of the 19th century, interest in the Museum revived after further vicissitudes and it was agreed that the collections should be transferred from the Society of Antiquaries to the Government, on condition that proper accommodation was provided for their free public exhibition. This took place in 1851, the year of the Great Exhibition in London's Crystal Palace, when public interest in 'the arts and manufactures' was high, and museums of industrial art and science were founded in the southern Capital. The contemporary concept of a museum as an institution inspiring good design lies behind the founding of the great Victoria and Albert Museum. The growth of the collections accelerated and there was a widening emphasis on Scottish history and antiquities. This development was fostered in particular by Joseph Anderson who was Keeper of the Museum from 1869 to 1913 and the dominating figure in Scottish archaeology over that long period. During his important career, he pieced Scottish prehistory into a coherent whole. However, with this growth of both prehistoric and historic collections came all the attendant problems of over-crowding and shortage of display and storage space. A fascinating series of photographs of the interior of the Museum about 1890 shows just how congested the displays had become, yet it still managed to attract 83,000 visitors that year (Plates 1 and 13).

This acute shortage of space has proved to be a continual headache right up to the present, and one which was only temporarily relieved when the Museum moved from the Mound to Queen Street in 1891. Although the gift of a new building was the generous gesture of Mr J R Findlay the proprietor of the *Scotsman* newspaper (he was persuaded to add the Museum to his gift for a National Portrait Gallery), the move from Princes Street drastically reduced attendances to a quarter and less. This was and still is a clear indication that Queen Street is not a central site though so close to the centre. It took

1. The Museum housed in the Royal Institution on the Mound, c 1890.

in fact about sixty years to build attendances back up to pre-1890 levels. Throughout the present century we have continued to add to the collections to such an extent that the increased space in the new Queen Street building was soon as hopelessly overcrowded as the Mound had been. This was one of the problems which led to a committee being appointed by the Secretary of State for Scotland in 1951 to report on the scope and function of the Museum. The Philip Report, named after Sheriff J R Philip, the chairman of the Committee, was accepted in 1952 and heralded a new phase in the Museum's development.

From the point of view of an interested public, the most important recommendation of the Philip Committee was that a central site should be obtained for a new Museum building which was accepted as the responsibility of government. Investigation of the possibilities began immediately and a site adjacent to the University area and the Royal Scottish Museum was proposed as suitable for a new permanent home for the Museum. This came to naught as described, though in no way crippling the National Museum itself. We should be thankful that an alternative scheme, a new home for the Burrell Collection in Glasgow, went ahead and now stands completed in the grounds of Pollok House.

For practical purposes the Museum has developed Sections to cater for the wide range of material in its collections. Until 1947, the specialisation necessary for a national museum was focussed on the prehistoric collections. Gestures had been made in the past towards systematically expanding in other areas but this was designed to develop the comparative approach in which 'modern' ethnological material could be seen to throw light on 'ancient' technology. There had never been a date limit on the material collected, but by creating a new curatorial post and in effect a new 'section' of the Museum, a deliberate direction was given to Museum policy to improve the balance of the collections by extending the areas of research and collecting into the 17th to 20th centuries. The 'modern' Section was then complemented in 1959 by the creation of a 'Country Life' Section with another curatorial post.

The medieval and 'modern' periods had been represented in the National Museum in an earlier era. In fact some very notable additions were made to the collections before the end of the 18th century. In 1796, the Museum was given a Covenanters' flag which had been carried at the battle of Bothwell Brig in 1679. Considering the circumstances of the time, the extreme repressive measures of fines and quartering of troops – notoriously the Highland Host in 1678 – followed by the conventiclers' victory over Claverhouse at Drumclog, the Covenanters' flag is not the brazen banner which might be expected. It is a white saltire with roses in the centre and the inscription 'For Religion, Covenants, King and Kingdomes', reminiscent of the spirit of a generation earlier, of the National Covenant in 1638 which had been a constitutional and not a revolutionary document. Such a flag may have more to tell us of the folk who fought for the Covenants in the reigns of Charles II and James VII. In *Old Mortality,* Scott paints a picture of dour, uncompromising extremists in the south west in 1679 and this tends to colour our view. Curiously, the same flag was refurbished briefly in 1745 and carried by the Edinburgh Volunteers. No doubt the design and inscription suited the uncertain or contradictory combination of sentiments then which inspired a short-lived local support of the Jacobite cause. The proscriptive legislation which was imposed after the '45 was only recently repealed and the French Revolutionary War had broken out when the flag came to the Museum. With the new popular democratic movements in an energetic phase and the establishment closing ranks – the act anent wrongeous imprisonment had just been suspended – it may have been felt that a man could be a man for a' that as long as he was in the National Museum. After all, Thomas Muir of Huntershill, tried for sedition in 1793 and transported, was himself a Fellow of the Society of Antiquaries and briefly a Curator of the Museum.

A second notable addition to the collections followed the Covenanters' flag a year later in the still uneasy atmosphere when the French 'Terror' was at its height. The worthy Buchan had written to the Lord Provost and Magistrates of the City in 1781 asking them for the Maiden when the Museum was founded. This hideous beheading machine or guillotine had been devised in Edinburgh in 1564 and, mercifully, had lain out of commission since 1697. The reputation of events in Paris must have persuaded the City Worthies to banish any idea of a comparison between judicial proceedings in the Athens of the North and the work of the *canaille* in that unruly Continental capital.

A broadening of the range of material collected by the National Museum is detectable in the late 1950s. The initiative for this came from the role adopted by the National Museum of creating and founding a national Scottish 'folk museum', a proposal of the Standing Commission on Museums and Galleries in 1949 and a recommendation of the Philip Committee in 1952. The Keeper could later report the acquisition of: 'Several rather humble objects of everyday use rescued from dwellings being demolished in various places will be appropriate for illustration of social and domestic history'. This varied from sections of the once ubiquitous box beds and building materials such as claut and clay partitions through to wooden locks, domestic utensils and hand tools. Of course, humble objects were not an invention of our own day in the Museum. In 1784, one of the early members of the Society of Antiquaries, Rev Donald Macintosh, presented to the collection a *cròcan* of wood used in the Hebrides for hanging pots over the fire. This insignificant but nonetheless important item is still in the Museum.

The breadth of interest of the Museum in trying to build up post-medieval and modern social history and agricultural collections without space to display them was reported and justified by the Keeper over twenty years ago. It would be a natural reaction to this approach to suggest that it is pointless to collect what we cannot display. It became obvious that the major advances in prehistoric archaeology had been due to the existence in museums of series of objects individually of little consequence which had been accumulated in order to preserve them. This had generally been done out of a sense of duty and with no idea of the information that could later be culled from them. It was similarly becoming obvious to those who were responsible for running the National Museum and for creating a national collection that informative displays of the still numerous objects only

recently out-dated and out-moded had to be based on collections whose significance would grow as they became larger. Over the last twenty years, the bulk of the accessions have belonged to this vital category of research collections, systematically developed for future as well as for present generations. The advantage of these modern objects as documents of social history over those of earlier ages is that it is often possible to gather with them information about how they were used or made, and by whom and where. Recorded information of this type becomes valued museum material and has to be stored and organised in the same way as the objects and the library.

This role of the National Museum was defined in 1962 and is as true, if not more true, now as then. Ironically, the pace of change and technological development accelerated in the 1960s and material collected then, although considered trivial, is already rare since what the National Museum was unable to accommodate has been disposed of and destroyed in the interim. What was commonplace a few years ago is now rare.

In the last twenty or thirty years, the emphasis in the study of history has moved away from political or constitutional history and the doings and sayings of great men towards social and economic history, and in re-examining the lives of our forefathers we have thrown the net wider in our search for source material. Characteristically, museums used to be the storehouses of relics and mementoes of great men. We are now more interested in trades and industries, in recognising home or commercially made materials for their native virtues, and in identifying when and how something was made, for whom and how it was used. The fact that it might be only a pale reflection of something made in London or Paris is merely a matter for passing comment rather than grounds for instant dismissal.

Attitudes in past generations towards material culture or the applied and decorative arts tended to be dominated by an exclusiveness. Thus a material of fine quality or manufacture might be assumed to be English or Continental, perhaps French or Italian. Anything else, such as

Scottish, for example, was provincial and inferior. A closer study of our own past and this fundamental change in the nature of historical studies has thankfully modified the bad old view. It may come as a relief to discover that fashions change in history as fashions change in dress – but not so quickly.

In many countries, museums provide a focus for national identity. The cynic will say that this is part of a conspiracy theory whereby the wayward provincial is weaned from separatism with a cultural anodyne. With enormous clarity of vision the Swede Artur Hazelius founded the Nordiska Museum in Stockholm in 1873 and followed it with his Swedish national open-air museum at Skansen in 1891. The industrial revolution was a later experience in Scandinavia than in Britain, and in the 1870s, the Swedes were sufficiently alive to the dynamic progress of contemporary change and the threat to society which, while growing wealthy, might lose sight of its roots.

In Britain, society has been more contemptuous of its traditions and customs, and less alive to the varieties of material and language. Effectively in Scotland we have used three languages, Scots, English and Gaelic. In spite of the irascible Dr Johnson's assertion that Gaelic had no literature, we know that Gaelic does have a very considerable literature, both rich and colourful and ancient. The illusion of 'Celtic gloom' and slow-moving, turgid emotions is totally foreign to Gaelic literature. It is an invention of the credulous 19th century English speaking world. We should also remember that in its earliest phase it was the first written vernacular in Europe. Too often we have failed to represent ourselves adequately and merely let ride the superficial judgements of outsiders. Perhaps these are generally below contempt but they are picked up by the observer and thrown back at us. While not undesirable, it may be denounced as distinctly unfashionable to create a focus of patriotic feeling. This might be all too readily confused with 'nationalism' as the scourge of Europe. Even if political nationalism has not identified itself with cultural nationalism, the latter has a positive role to play in creating and fostering national consciousness. Eyebrows and defence mechanisms would doubtless be

triggered into action if this were to appear as an aggressive cultural nationalism. There have been scholarly attempts to do this in the past, and the National Museum has taken the initiative in fostering the idea of the value of Scottish identity. Since the Union in 1707, a feeling for national identity has ebbed and flowed, and although it has often adopted a political guise, it has as often used the pen rather than the sword. Language and literature are the strongest indicators of the health or decline of nationhood. Sometimes a battle with political overtones was fought out through the medium of literature. Scott and MacDiarmid are different expressions of this. MacDiarmid's honest radicalism and braid Scots are nearer us and more familiar. What was Scott's contribution? The story can be briefly told.

When the Government proposed to reform the banking system by forbidding banks to issue their own notes in 1826, there was an outcry in Scotland where the problems of failing banks had not been so acute as in England. Indeed, Scottish banks' credit was good and small notes were an essential because of a lack of gold and silver. Such a measure proposed in London was also a flagrant violation of the Act of Union. Those who argued rather less with rationality than with emotion warned of an assertion of English power and a reduction to uniformity in the currency. When we survey the wealth of artistry, detail and fine engraving which was absorbed in Scottish notes, we too can understand the contemporary emotional reaction. Scott joined the denunciation of the Government's scheme and rapidly penned the sensational *Letters of Malachi Malagrowther* which he thought would 'light on some ingredients of national feeling and set folk's beards in a blaze – and so much the better if it does – I mean better for Scotland . . .'. There was indeed no trouble with the note issue, the banks were well capitalised and they freely accepted each others' notes. As the patriot Malachi rightly complained, Scotland was being made a whipping boy for the faults of others. Such was the outcry stimulated by the *Letters* that the Government backed down and abandoned the measure. At its most bland, the Wizard Scott provides an artistic justification for Scottish consciousness. He was in his own time an old Tory among the Radicals but

2. Breast star of 'The Most Ancient and Most Noble Order of the Thistle', made of silver, gold and enamels and set with rose diamonds, by a London jeweller, T Wirgman, c1805-11.

4. Silver gilt work-box set with cut and polished semi-precious stones. It is fitted inside with writing and sewing implements, including a penknife, a seal monogrammed 'JB' and a vinaigrette. Made in Edinburgh, possibly by M Crichton, c1870.

5. This medallion is cut from the semi-precious stone citrine to commemorate the visit of George IV to Scotland in 1822. The obverse bears the laureate head of the King, surrounded by a wreath of thistles and a ribbon inscribed 'GOD SAVE THE KING'. The reverse shows a view of Edinburgh Castle and is inscribed 'IN COMMEMORATION/OF THE ROYAL VISIT/TO SCOTLAND 1822'.

3. Spinning wheel and reel or yarn winder made c1829 by John Watson, Bristo Port, Edinburgh. Each piece has an inscribed brass plate recording that it was made as a 'love gift' by John Watson for his daughter and it has passed from mother to daughter in the same family since then.

6. Locket, made of gold, enamelled and set with seed pearls and miniatures which may represent Mary, Queen of Scots and James VI her son.

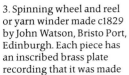

7. White painted oak double bay bookcase with leaded glass doors decorated with a simple design of leaves and stems. Designed by Charles Rennie Mackintosh for Dunglass Castle, Bowling.

8. Oak barrel-lidded rug chest with an inlaid marquetry panel depicting a fox-hunting scene. Designed by Sir Robert Lorimer, early 20th century.

9 and 10. Oak and walnut sideboard or serving table with three drawers, barley twist legs and fine backpanel of intricate carved tracery of monkeys and pigs. Designed by Sir Robert Lorimer, early 20th century.

11. Pair of corner armchairs with leather upholstery and gracefully carved, almost heart-shaped splats. Designed by Sir Robert Lorimer, early 20th century.

12. Oak display cabinet with shaped shelves and carved scroll mouldings on the cornice. Thought to be inspired by the French furniture of Louis XVI. Designed by Sir Robert Lorimer, early 20th century.

his plea is timeless: 'What makes Scotland Scotland need not be lost'.

From time to time in the past, the Museum or its parent Society had no reservations in proposing the national collections as a focus of patriotic sentiment. The energetic Secretary of the Society of Antiquaries, Daniel Wilson, was to use archaeological studies as his way to the hearts of the people. By the mid 19th century, Scott had been dead for almost two decades and his proposition of Scottish national identity was fading. Wilson wanted to create a wider popular interest in archaeology and through the National Museum and his own writings to generate patriotism; he took as his model the Scandinavian and especially the Danish example, both for its popular and patriotic appeal and also for its concepts of prehistoric development. Without alluding to it as such, he seemed to be recalling the cultural consequences of the Union of the Crowns in 1603 when the king, court and nobility moved away south. Wilson complained that: 'our native nobility have stood aloof from us . . . we mourn the decay of the old generous spirit of nationality, which is evinced by the array of names of our nobility, members of Parliament, and Scottish gentry figuring in the lists of the more fashionable Societies of London'. Perhaps in reality he saw the loss of potential subscriptions. Why join those Societies down there while you can join ours?

Under the direction of men such as Daniel Wilson and Joseph Anderson in the second half of the 19th century, it was clear that the Keeper of the Museum had to be more than a Custodian. He had to organise the collections in a comprehensive way, to explain them and to interpret them. This of course has a modern ring to it. 'Interpretation' has been the recent buzz-word in museums, the common currency of museum curators today, the reflective reflex of 1880 and the obsession of 1980. In practical terms and briefly, we should understand by 'interpretation', the display and arrangement of the museum collection in such a way as to convey and explain the meaning and significance of the material and its place in time and space. Obviously this is part of the Museum's contribution to education, hopefully avoiding the pitfalls of stunning the visitor and of stifling

interest or even fun. History after all should not be dull. It is widely enjoyed in one form and another, it amounts to a minor industry and like every good industry, it has something for everybody. In a memorable passage, a leading British historian suggested the purpose of studying the past: 'The future is dark, the present burdensome; only the past, dead and finished bears contemplation . . . The desire to know what went before, the desire to understand the passage down time, these are common human attributes'.

In an age when communication is rated so highly, museums are in the business to interpret and communicate the past and even to leaven the dullness of history. It is certainly a common fault to prejudge the past without learning about it. A typical attitude for example is the assumption that the remote past was barbaric and inferior.

Our remote ancestors certainly had different ways of looking at the world but on the whole, their senses and emotions were stimulated and satisfied in much the same way as our own. They were no more savages than we are. If we think carefully about what fills the horizons of our minds – canned entertainment, television, beer and sport perhaps – taste, temperament and ideological bent and their infinite variety are not easily satisfied. It may often be difficult to devise an attractive and entertaining view of Scotland's historical and archaeological heritage. The museum may not inspire excitement readily. The glass cases of old may be daunting. Given that we have to preserve as well as display, the separation of object and viewer is a necessary evil for which no remedy has yet been offered.

So how does a certain object come to be behind glass in the Museum? What magic ritual or mysterious process puts it there? Several questions may be prompted by this sort of reflection. What is it? Why is it important? We read a label to find out. In the past the labels in museums tended to proffer little more than the name of the donor, perhaps a noble patron. We saluted his generosity and his wisdom and thought twice about the magnanimity of his gesture. Today, the name of the donor gets a nod at the bottom of an interpretive text. This is not disrespect. There is an attempt within the narrow compass of a few words to set our object in its social and historical context. Why is it there? By implication, it becomes imbued behind glass with an aura of value, automatically equated with riches beyond avarice. But the reasoning behind this ready indentification may be *ex post facto* – not so much it's there because it's valuable, but rather it's valuable because it's there. We cannot fault this after all. This amounts to a tribute to the Museum's sense of discrimination and choice. It may be there due to a sense of values widely recognised or it may be there because the Museum has applied scholarly research and other tests, and measured the object against our view of the past. Senses of value may in this case be highly individual and it reflects the thought and understanding of museum curators. How then is the decision made to acquire an object?

The National Museum may sometimes be considered to be modest about its achievements in this respect. The renewal of interest in Art Nouveau and the undervalued work of Charles Rennie Mackintosh was a feature of art appreciation in the late 1960s. As early as 1959, the Keeper of the Museum could report the purchase of furniture and decorative fittings designed by Charles Rennie Mackintosh and members of the Glasgow School. Innovative collecting such as this generally has to be by way of purchase in that by definition, the material is not regarded as collectable or valuable by the interested public who will tend to have their own firm ideas as to what could or should be in a museum or what they would consider donating. If they themselves do not value the object or have no standards of recognised taste against which to judge it, then they will underrate the act of donation.

Mackintosh had never been truly in vogue even during the woefully short period of his local success in Glasgow. But as a disciple or a pioneer of the modern European movement in architecture and design he was recognised, as his work came to be known outwith Scotland, as the leading exponent of a distinctive style of Art Nouveau; this was dubbed 'the Glasgow style', although in Glasgow itself those locals who recognised something different cautiously described it as 'artistic'. If the rest of his countrymen steadfastly refused even to accord it this modest merit, it took more than half a

century for these talents to be fairly lionised. In 1968, to celebrate the centenary of his birth, the Scottish Arts Council staged an exhibition of Mackintosh's architecture, design and painting successively in the Royal Scottish Museum and in the Victoria and Albert Museum.

The time was ripe for a fashionable re-appraisal of Art Nouveau and Charles Rennie Mackintosh and within a few years, Mackintosh became very popular and his work and the work of the Glasgow School were commanding high prices on the market. In fact pieces which the National Museum had secured for sums of ten or twenty pounds can now be said to be worth more than ten or twenty thousand pounds.

The bulk of Mackintosh's surviving work now belongs appropriately to the Glasgow School of Art, Mackintosh's own magnificent creation, and to Glasgow University. Much of this was his work for public clients and for example for the celebrated Glasgow tea rooms of Miss Cranston in Sauchiehall Street, Ingram Street and Argyle Street. It is essential that the leading museums for whom celebration of Mackintosh is appropriate do not find themselves competing for ownership of his work. The National Museum has respected the interests of the other museums and has concentrated on his private work, domestic designs for himself and his family and friends. This may not have the same prestige as his work for public display but it has the unselfconscious charm of Mackintosh's artistic convictions translated into domestic informality.

The first piece of Mackintosh's domestic furniture acquired by the National Museum was a hall settle in oak with a beaten lead panel and linen seat covers made about 1895 by Guthrie and Wells of Glasgow. This piece was made for the Macdonald family, Mackintosh's future parents-in-law, at Dunglass Castle, Dumbartonshire. Curiously, in spite of a perverse disregard for the Glasgow School's work in London, this settle was accepted for the London Arts and Crafts Exhibition of 1896. The arts and crafts movement in the south conspired to exclude or to bring into disrepute the radical modernity of the Scotto-Continental school. The settle in common with other examples of Mackintosh's work shows a strong affinity with the vernacular tradition. This is part of the attraction of the Glasgow School and especially Mackintosh in that, in their revolt against artistic conventions, they drew on Scottish indigenous styles for inspiration and Celtic motifs, contemporaneously popular though spurious or modern.

The National Museum therefore has to set the pace individually from its staff's researches and independently of market forces and fashion. If we choose to display bed pans rather than gold and frankincense, then a serious point is being made and certainly not a flippant one. The staff investigate the intrinsic characteristics of objects such as the medium or material and the method of manufacture. If it is made of base or precious metals for example, this would be considered significant but perhaps not the overriding factor. This process might be carried out exclusively by the research and conservation laboratories. The curatorial staff investigate the historical background and come up with either extraordinary circumstances such as the association with certain people or events, or ordinary circumstances such as reflect ways of life and work in Scotland in the past.

The value of donations and purchases may be recognised by an insurance valuation or a purchase price. In other words, the value is expressed bluntly in monetary terms. The Museum has to express the value in different terms although the curious may be titillated by gazing on museum objects as in a shop window, each item merely supporting a price ticket. This would at least be practicable with the acquisitions of the last decade where the purchase prices would still be meaningful.

What would we do with our national treasures if we had to price them? Such priceless relics as the 'Galloway Mazer', the 16th century Renaissance standing bowl, was bought in 1954 in far from easy circumstances. It was made by the silversmith James Gray in the Canongate for Archibald Stewart and his wife Ellen Acheson and is dated 1569. The Museum bid for it in March 1954 but was not successful. Subsequently its export by an American museum was prohibited by the Export of Works of Art Reviewing Committee and with a generous parliamentary grant the Museum was able to purchase the Mazer for £11,500. Other Scottish institutions had decided not to bid for this because of other

priorities as well as presumably of cost. The National Museum clearly had a recognised responsibility for collecting Scottish domestic silver and this policy has been adhered to firmly over the ensuing thirty years. The Galloway Mazer was bought for a king's ransom thirty years ago. How could we price it today? So many of our treasures are beyond price and it can be said to be an irrelevance to try to put prices on them.

Philosophies on running museums are many and colourful. They might concern the obvious questions such as what to collect and why; these are not necessarily as simple as they sound. We consider what to select and preserve and what to dismiss. We may then be forced to reconsider. We also have to consider what to restore rather than to merely conserve and how much to restore. Often these philosophical dilemmas are solved pragmatically if unsatisfactorily. A museum may not have the funds to embark on a painstaking and lengthy process of restoration.

The story is told in museums, perhaps it is apocryphal, of the professional curator from a British national museum marvelling at some rare piece, say of the status of the Warwick vase, in a Continental museum. Why had he not known of it before? Was it published in some learned archaeological journal? No, because as it gradually dawned on him, the piece was almost a fake. The conservation laboratory of the particular museum had built up the pot conjecturally or even one might say imaginatively from a fragment of excavated terra cotta. The next twist in the tale is a theoretical one like the presentation of the pot. One could bet that the majority of the visiting public would be more impressed by the restored pot than the lone fragment. The agonising over conjectural restoration is more or less exclusive to the museum profession, the real sanction being the judgement of their professional heirs and successors.

The problems of running museums are both practical and philosophical. A limited amount of space has to be managed and manipulated by a limited manpower with limited financial resources. Scottish history, in common with any other kind of history, suffers from two distinct shortcomings, scholarly manpower and finance, both owing their origins to a well-known public attitude – indifference to the national history or indifference to Scottish as distinct from 'British History'. Specialisation within the field therefore seems foolhardy when funds are hard to acquire, and yet specialised research and publication are the life-blood of an institution such as ours.

Museums, and especially the national museums, have for long traditionally generated formidable works of research. The National Museum for example has played a leading part in archaeological research in Scotland, in Britain and even in Europe. Since 1851, members of staff have regularly contributed to the *Proceedings of the Society of Antiquaries of Scotland* which have continued in an unbroken run to the present day, the latest published volume of *Proceedings* for 1982 being Volume 112 and running to 677 pages. This journal is a goldmine of information not only on archaeology but also on Scottish ethnology and material culture. 1851 was an important year in the development of the National Museum for not only were the collections transferred to state ownership, but also the scholar Sir Daniel Wilson produced his influential *Archaeology and prehistoric annals of Scotland*. At a stroke, he

13. Joseph Anderson, Keeper of the Museum, c 1890.

revolutionised the study of Scottish archaeology and deeply influenced the development of British archaeology, and incidentally introduced the word 'prehistoric' into the English language. From time to time, the opportunity arises to produce a monograph on museum material that by its nature and quality becomes an indispensable link in the study of British archaeology. Such is the two volume study of the St Ninian's Isle treasure of silver objects discovered during an excavation of an ecclesiastical site on this Shetland island in 1958.

Although we would hesitate to attempt to redefine 'treasure', we all recognise that in this modern age, treasure signifies wealth which is measured in terms of money. Both riches and poverty are now valued in terms of money. Some centuries ago treasure might be not only precious metal but also wealth in material terms; the word for 'treasure' in Gaelic is *eudail* which also meant 'cattle'. In a heroic society, treasure was possessions on the hoof. The criteria against which we might measure value may vary from intrinsic value to antiquity and rarity. Treasure is anything which is valued and it is part of the role of the Museum to store up treasure and to define what is treasure for our own and future generations.

In the following sections, we illustrate some of the treasures acquired in recent years, indicating how we have added to the nation's treasures already accumulated and how we have moved on to new pastures and redefined our own view of the past and its treasures. In a ringing statement, the redoutable Joseph Anderson stated his conviction of why the work of the National Museum should go on: 'We know that the history of Scotland is not the history of any other nation on earth, and that if her records were destroyed, it would matter nothing to us that all the records of all other nations were preserved. They could neither tell the story of our ancestors, nor restore the lost links in the development of our culture and civilisation'.

Ten years is not a long time in the life of a national museum or gallery. Ten years is not a long time in the already long existence of the National Museum of Antiquities of Scotland. Founded in 1781 and surviving many misfortunes, this National Museum is still going strong.

Furniture

The National Museum's furniture collection has expanded rapidly during the past ten years. Furniture and fittings have always been an important element in the Museum's interests although early examples, that is earlier than the 17th century, are rare both within and outwith the Museum. The sad lack of early pieces is further complicated by the fact that it can be very difficult to give an exact provenance to early furniture. As both Scottish and English makers were influenced by the same ideas from abroad, most notably from the Low Countries, and as the Scots tended to copy styles fashionable amongst their richer English contemporaries, the tendency was to produce very similar work.

During the early years of this century, the Museum amassed a collection of chairs, mainly because they were small, portable and easily stored. A fine example of this early policy, is the 17th century Douglas genealogical chair. The chair lists the lineage of a branch of the Douglas family, the earliest decipherable date being 1057. The crest and heraldry on the back panel show it was made for Sir William Douglas of Glenbervie and his wife Anne and can be dated to 1665. This practice of embellishing family items with crests seems to have been a common feature in the 17th century and indeed can be found not only on furniture but also on mantelshelves and over door lintels.

A collecting policy has been evolved by the Museum, especially during the last thirty years, to identify Scottish furniture, to pinpoint regional variations, to acquire a variety of pieces and regional designs and also the work of known makers, both joiners and cabinet-makers. The result has been to establish an extensive and comprehensive selection of 19th and 20th century furniture in the Museum. Not only does the collection reflect the outside influences affecting Scottish furniture makers, but also reveals the individuality of design and craftsmanship which became the hallmark of designers such as Sir Robert Lorimer and Charles Rennie Mackintosh in the late 19th and early 20th centuries.

A single item of furniture can often provide the student with a number of interesting facts. Not only can it give us an insight into the fashion and tastes of the day, but it can also give a fascinating glimpse into the history surrounding the making of an individual piece and can allow us to set it into the wider historical perspective. An advantage to be gained from museum presentation is the gathering together of functions in material culture which generally in practice have become separated. Thus we can juxtapose the work of designer, maker or craftsman and user. A good example of the many facets to be illuminated in museum display is a mahogany clothes press which is not only a

14. Oak and walnut veneered tallboy or chest of drawers with ten graded drawers, each with mouldings of geometrical design. Interestingly, this piece is signed inside by its maker, G. Fettes, as his 'apprentice piece' – 'made by G. Fettes, 1913, 1st June, 4th year of his apprentice'. Designed by Sir Robert Lorimer.

15. Jacobean-style chest of drawers in oak and walnut veneer with geometric mouldings on the drawers.

16. Burr walnut and oak, two drawer, dressing table with barley sugar twist legs and shaped stretcher. Designed by Sir Robert Lorimer. Early 20th century.

fine example of 18th century cabinet-making, but is also notable in that it was made in 1786 by Deacon William Brodie, the sinister inspiration for Stevenson's *Dr Jekyll and Mr Hyde.* We also know for whom the press was made for inside one of the doors is carved 'made by William Brodie for Jean Wilson . . . Canongate 1786'. This practice of carving or writing the makers name in furniture can provide us today with a number of interesting facts. Over one hundred years later we have a further example inside an oak and walnut tallboy, designed by Sir Robert Lorimer, and made by 'G. Fettes 1913, 1st June, 4th year of his apprentice'. This tallboy not only gives us the name of the individual maker, but also a fascinating insight into the structure of the craft guild which governed furniture makers and its strict laws of apprenticeship.

Undoubtedly, there are fine examples of 17th and 18th century furniture in the Museum, such as the Traill four-poster bed, intricately carved and inlaid, bearing the Arms of the Traills of Fife and Orkney and dated 1641. However the full

17. Oak linen press with moulded cornice above a pair of linenfold panelled doors, carved with the initials RWRM and JRSM. R. W. R. Mackenzie bought Earlshall in 1890 and commissioned Lorimer to restore it. The press is attributed to Sir Robert Lorimer and was probably made by Whytock and Reid.

burgeoning of the collection comes with the 19th century, and the Museum has been fortunate in acquiring significant examples of the changing modes and styles of the day. These styles range from the traditionalist approach of Sir Robert Lorimer and his followers, to the modernistic and experimental furniture of C. R. Mackintosh and his contemporaries. Over the past twenty five years, the Museum's collection of Mackintosh furniture has grown considerably with a number of items, amongst which are the pieces specifically designed for Dunglass Castle, Dumbartonshire, the home of his wife's family. The finest example is a white painted oak bookcase with double bay doors decorated with leaded glass and a simple design of leaves and stems (Plate 7). We have also found examples of other exponents of the modernist style. A fine oak sidebaord by E. A. Taylor of Glasgow, (1874-1952) shows the Art Nouveau style at its finest, with inlaid stylised roses and brass mounted handles and lockplates (Plate 23), while a mahogany dining suite designed c1903 by Adam Galt of Edinburgh is characterised by a delicate inlaid chequered banding. The sideboard also carries a lovely example of stained glass work which was such a popular medium at the time, using stylised birds and flowers (Plates 20-22).

This modernist style co-existed side by side with the more traditional approach which looked for its inspiration to the past. In the past three years, the National Museum has established an extensive and representative collection of furniture by one of the most widely admired exponents of the traditionalist style, Sir Robert Lorimer. The material came from two houses in Fife which he refurbished, Earlshall and Gibliston House. In addition to furniture, the Museum has examples of the ironwork designed by Lorimer and made by blacksmiths in Fife and Edinburgh, and textile designs and plans for interior decorating. All this material complements the vast archive of Lorimer's work held by the Royal Commission on the Ancient and Historical Monuments of Scotland which occupies Lorimer's old Edinburgh office at 54 Melville Street.

Many of the revivalist styles of 19th century Britain are now lumped together as 'Gothic revival' or 'neo-Gothic' and often considered to be monuments of ugliness, extravagance and bad taste. The Romantic revival in Scotland took some time to find a particularly Scottish identity and busied itself for a generation or more with the excesses of the English Gothic. We can lament now that it did not seek out and develop the Scottish vernacular traits of the 16th and 17th centuries. The Scottish expression of neo-Gothic architecture is sometimes termed 'Scottish baronial' and its

18. Oak armchair with drawer underneath and shaped backsplats, reminiscent of the 'medieval' style. Designed by Sir Robert Lorimer. Early 20th century.

19. Oak single bed with linenfold headboard and two headposts, carved in the form of two small figures, reputedly the work of the Clow Brothers. Designed by Sir Robert Lorimer. Early 20th century.

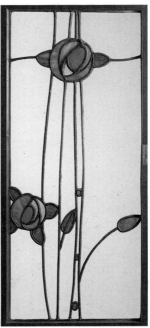

20-22. Mahogany sideboard, designed by Adam Galt, c1903. The upper portion has leaded glass doors executed in Art Nouveau style with birds and flowers and also brass handles and lockplates.

23. Oak sideboard with inlaid stylised roses and brass mounted handles and lockplates. Made by Wylie and Lochhead to a design by E A Taylor.

26. Goblets of emerald green glass with fluted bowls, possibly from Leith, late 18th century.

24. A selection of trade bottles from breweries and carbonated-water works, including a 'codd' bottle with a 'marble' as a stopper, and an egg-shaped 'hamilton'.

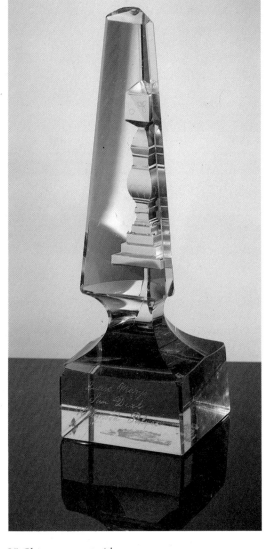

25. Glass ornament with the shape of the Queen Mary Sundial at Holyrood Palace cut out from the rear, giving a three dimensional effect.

final leavening into a more gentle edition of its late 19th century work was at the hands of Lorimer. He developed the final flowering of the Scots Baronial tradition within his own appreciation of the workmanship and materials to be found in the Scots late medieval and vernacular traditions. A fine example of the influence of past styles on Lorimer's work is an oak linen press, recently purchased from Earlshall (Plate 17). Although dating from the early 20th century, the press has heavily carved linenfold doors, more reminiscent of Jacobean times, as is the carved lintel below the cornice, bearing the initials of the then owners of Earlshall, Mr and Mrs R. W. R. MacKenzie who commissioned Lorimer to refurbish the house when they bought it in 1890.

One of the more important influences on Lorimer was Kellie Castle near Pittenweem. His father took a long lease of it in 1878, and the family set about restoring what amounted to a derelict building consisting of a 14th century keep with additions of the 15th to 17th centuries. The prevailing fashion in the late 19th century for treating old buildings was to rebuild them in extravagant taste and manner. The Lorimers embarked on and virtually pioneered the interest in repairing old buildings and restoring their character in a conscious effort not to change it. History had become the major force in building design and was to shape tastes in furnishings and fittings. History and Kellie were the influence and inspiration of Lorimer's love of the Scottish Baronial style.

Charles Rennie Mackintosh, like Lorimer, not only involved himself in furniture design. Both men worked with the total concept approach to a property, designing everything from the house itself to the smallest fitting. However, whereas Lorimer designs were firmly linked to the past creating heavy, well made craft pieces of furniture, Mackintosh's vision was

27. Elm dresser with four graded and shaped shelves, below which is a marquetry panel depicting a stag-hunting scene. Designed by Sir Robert Lorimer and made by Whytock and Reid.

28. Mahogany bureau-cabinet with moulded cornices and six assorted sized drawers. Designed and used by Sir Robert Lorimer, it was kept in his home in Melville Street, Edinburgh. A fine example of the work of Whytock and Reid. Early 20th century.

experimental, using forms and materials often with little regard to their durability.

Less claims have been made in recent years for Sir Robert Lorimer than for Charles Rennie Mackintosh, not least on their own native heath. Nevertheless, in his own day, Lorimer was Scotland's foremost architect while Mackintosh died forgotten and furth of Scotland. At the distance of half a century or more, the respective merits of these two men can be more easily appreciated. It is undeniable that both Lorimer and Mackintosh had a profound influence on the design and tastes of their day, both at home and abroad. It is not our place to comment on the merits of one over the other as both had a separate vision and therefore worked towards different ends. The Museum has however been fortunate in acquiring significant examples of the work of both men, thus affording those interested with an opportunity of judging for themselves.

In recent years a small collection has been built up of bothy furniture and working men's clothes- and meal-chests, with a fine Orkney straw chair as another feature. This recent development has added a further dimension to the furniture collection which now covers an even wider spectrum, giving a comprehensive picture of the range of furniture and makers at work in Scotland at all levels of society throughout the centuries.

Pottery and Glass

Pottery and glass form two important parts of our collection in the Museum. This is not only because the objects often have a strong visual appeal, but because the histories of the two industries were pointers to Scotland's economic, political and social past.

Even the humble beer bottle can be of importance. Bottles of one sort or another have been produced in Scotland since the 17th century, but even modern 'empties' can tell a tale of more than a pleasantly convivial evening. Often they have the name of a brewery or an 'aerated water' works moulded or sandblasted on their sides, and may, for instance, be our only record of many small industries which flourished in Scotland at one time or another, as well as of the drinking habits of our forbears (Plate 24).

Wine and ale drinkers usually, of course, require glasses to drink from, and glasses and goblets are the kind of simple, functional objects which often display the decorative skill of their maker to its best advantage. A set of late 18th century wine glasses, which are thought to have been made in Leith, with their boldly 'wrythen' bowls illustrate this point beautifully (Plate 29). A glass 'rummer' or large goblet, probably made in Edinburgh c1840, shows a more elaborate and very different style of decoration (Plate 30). The base, stem and lower bowl were cut, giving a brilliant

29. A wine glass with baluster stem and wrythen bowl perhaps made by the Edinburgh and Leith Glassworks Company in the late 18th century.

sparkle but the upper part was skillfully copper-wheel engraved with a dashing scene of coach and horses, as well as the monogram of its owner. It must have been a prized possession, along with its twin which is now in Huntly House Museum, Edinburgh.

Engraving is a highly skilled craft, and it is always interesting to know something of the men whose skills survive in their products to give us so much pleasure today. The Museum owns several pieces which were engraved in Scotland by a family of Bohemian origin. Emanuel Lerche arrived in Scotland in 1853, moving to Alloa in 1873, where he and his son Stephen produced many beautiful engraved designs, often of fabulous complexity, on decanters, goblets and jugs (Plates 31-33).

Glasses and decanters with their convivial associations are often decorated with toasts and other commands to 'drink and be merry'. These inscriptions can give interesting clues as to what was uppermost in the drinker's mind, like the patriotic toast engraved on a decanter from a house in the Borders – 'The Land We Live In' (Plate 34). Others ensured that a good time would be had by all, in words – and music – like the inscriptions on a set of large covered goblets of early 19th century date which belonged to the Edinburgh Society of Musicians (Plate 35). Even one of the glasses engraved by the Lerche family has a design of barley and hops, which would have been frowned on by the Victorian Temperance Societies! (Plate 36).

Glass, like pottery, has always been a favourite material for souvenirs and other little ornaments (Plate 25). This may be partly because superstitions have been

31. A pair of decanters engraved with a design of herons and palm trees, by Stephen Lerche.

32. These goblets were engraved by Emanuel Lerche, the donor's grandfather, who came to Scotland from Bohemia in 1853. They show Holyrood Palace and are also monogrammed with his initials.

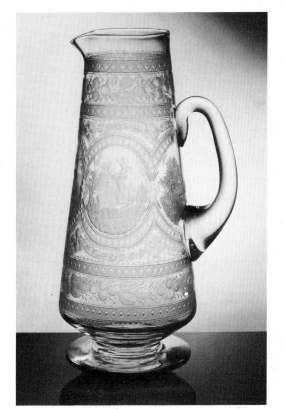

33. A water jug engraved in Alloa by Stephen Lerche.

30. *Opposite:* A cut and engraved 'rummer' which bears the initials 'IML'. Possibly Edinburgh, c1840.

34. This decanter is engraved with the owner's initials and a patriotic motto. The rings round the neck act as finger grips and are often seen on decanters like this of early 19th century date.

attached to it, especially among seafaring and fishing communities. Glass novelties, called 'friggers' have often been produced at glassworks as were the sceptres, canes, badges, and even musical instruments

which were carried in the annual trades processions of the glass makers during the 19th century. The Museum has been given three miniature bugles of green glass which were possibly mementoes of such an

35. One of a set of three covered goblets all engraved with poetry and scenes of music-making.

36. A goblet engraved by one of the Lerche family, with sprays of barley and hops.

37. These little bugles of different shades of green glass were made as novelties, possibly at Prestonpans.

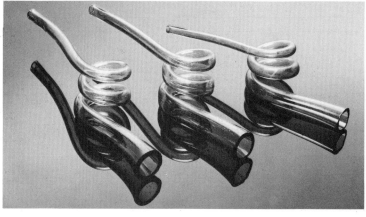

38. *Opposite:* A pair of hand painted porcelain figures from West Pans, c1770.

occasion.

Ceramic production in Scotland on an industrial basis got off to rather a later start than large-scale glass making. One of the earlier potteries at West Pans (near Musselburgh) produced very finely decorated porcelain in the last half of the 18th century whose detail and colour rival the best of English porcelain decoration at that time (Plate 38). This sort of ware satisfied the tastes of the richer Scottish customer whose family might already own an entire dinner service of porcelain decorated with their armorial bearings imported from China. Many pieces of Chinese armorial porcelain, from various Scottish families, have been acquired by the Museum, and form a material reminder of the strong trading links which existed between 18th century Scotland and the Far East.

By the 19th century a large industry had grown up, manufacturing mostly earthenware and stoneware. Like the glass industry, it was concentrated in areas where raw materials occurred naturally or could easily be shipped in, like Glasgow, Fife and the south shore of the Firth of Forth. Like glass, pottery was popular in humble as well as grand homes, providing a splash of colour on many a mantelpiece and dresser. 'Transfer' printing and hand-painting, (often along with 'sponge' printing) emerged as the two major forms of decoration, although beautifully executed moulding and 'sprigging' could transform a humble salt-glazed 'saut bucket' probably from the Caledonian Pottery, Glasgow, into a spectacular work of art (Plate 39).

Meanwhile, the tradition of hand-painting, which had vividly decorated many

39. This 'saut bucket' may
have been made as a
wedding or betrothal gift
for 'Andrew & Janet Boswell
1854' possibly by the
Caledonian Pottery. On
loan from M. J. Watson.

pieces of the East Coast and Fife pottery,
evolved under the direction of the
Bohemian decorator Karel Nekola from 1883
onwards, into the characteristic Wemyss
ware style produced at Robert Heron and
Son's Fife Pottery. This brilliantly coloured
ware with its nature-inspired designs is as
much sought after by antique collectors
today as it was by the fashionable in the
1880s and 90s, and the Museum owns a good
selection of representative pieces (Plate 56).

Another factory which produced
very individualistic 'art' pottery during the
late 19th century was that at Dunmore
owned by Peter Gardiner. The beautiful
glazes and exotic shapes of Dunmore pieces
are their most characteristic features (Plate
40). Dunmore is situated very close to Alloa
and a teapot in our collection comes from
the Alloa Pottery. Its deep, shiny glaze has
been copper-wheel engraved as if it were
glass, into a beautiful design of ferns and
twigs. This was probably done by Stephen
Lerche who, like his father Emanuel, was
master engraver at the Pottery. As we have
already seen, they were both also
accomplished glass engravers, and this
illustrates the close connections and fruitful
cross-fertilization that existed between the
glass and pottery industries. Transfer
printing was, however probably the most
popular form of pottery decoration, and this
kind of ware was produced all over Scotland,
usually in blue and white. Much of it was
very finely executed like a bowl thought to
be from Rathbones, Portobello (Plate 41).
Several of the main producers were based in
Glasgow and the best known and largest of
these was the firm of J & M P Bell & Co (or
J & M P Bell & Co Ltd as it later became).
Their output was extremely wide-ranging,

40. A wart-covered toad from Dunmore which really serves a function as a hanging wall-vase.

41. A blue and white transfer printed bowl which is probably from Rathbones Pottery, Portobello.

but one of their most interesting activities has come to light in a collection of plates which was amassed in South East Asia. It seems from this that Bells, as well as other Scottish potteries, were exporting pottery in large quantities during the second half of the 19th century. Bells in particular, developed a range of designs specially geared to the Eastern market. These were based on oriental motifs and subjects and were printed in two bright, contrasting colours. They then named these designs using the local language. 'Johore'

'Buah-buah' and 'Burung Kupu' give a hint of something a far cry from the smokey, industrial Victorian Glasgow where the plates began their journey – reversing the trend begun more than a century previously by the Chinese makers of armorial porcelain! Now the Scottish plates have returned to their country of origin to be kept in the Museum as example of the commercial drive and industrial skill of their enterprising Victorian manufacturers (Plate 55).

42. A teapot from the Alloa Pottery engraved with foliage and his initials by Stephen Lerche, the donor's father.

Silver and Pewter

Antique silver always seems to be the yardstick against which the concept of national 'treasure' is measured. As silver can easily be given a financial value, and because people have become accustomed to reading press reports of some important pieces making huge prices at auction, it is all too easy to equate importance solely with value. It cost 'x' thousand pounds therefore it must be important! While we cannot ignore this equation, and as the Museum is dependent on public money for its purchase grant we are constantly aware of just how expensive some objects have become. We are however more interested in placing Scottish silver firmly in its social and historical context. Before we consider buying a piece the questions we ask first are: who made it and when, what was it used for and who was it for. We have emphasised that we buy silver, for although we have always accepted donations (and still do), since 1963 when we began a systematic attempt to form a representative collection of Scottish silver, purchase has had to be the main means of acquisition.

Our collection attempts to cover as wide a stylistic, chronological and geographical range as possible. We have also tried to collect with firm reference to the documentary source material that is available. For example, we have built up a large archive of known and unknown makers' marks from all over Scotland, and we also have files of references to silversmiths and their wares in contemporary documents. In this way we have been able to build up a picture of the role of silver and silversmiths in Scottish social history. It has also been possible to look at artistic development and the taste and requirements of the Scottish public from the late 17th century to the early 20th century, by collecting as many different items of table and other domestic silver as possible.

From at least the 16th century silversmiths were based mainly in the towns and burghs of Scotland, and by c1700 places such as Aberdeen, Glasgow, Dundee, Inverness and Perth each had several working silversmiths. They were all organised as part of the Hammermen's guild, which included all craftsmen who used a hammer in their trade, and whose motto was 'By Hammer and Hand all Arts do Stand'. Normally burgh silversmiths (or goldsmiths, the terms were interchangeable as they worked with both precious metals) stamped their own personal mark and the town mark on their wares. Town marks were often taken from an element in their coats of Arms: the Glasgow mark was the tree, fish and bell, Inverness used a dromedary, Dundee, a pot of lilies and Perth a two headed eagle. Unfortunately most provincial craftsmen never developed a systematized scheme for stamping silver with date-letters, and thus accurately dating their ware is often difficult. (An Assay Office was set up in Glasgow in 1819 and from then until 1964, when it shut down, all Glasgow silver had to have a date-letter mark). Our collection reflects this widespread geographical distribution of silversmiths, and we have objects made in towns from Wick to Dumfries. We also illustrate the types of pieces produced by provincial makers. In the larger centres of population the craftsmen developed a wide range of products, from teaspoons to complete tea services, while in the smaller burghs they tended to concentrate on smaller workaday items such as tea and tablespoons. (The generic term for all cutlery, including teaspoons, tablespoons, knives, forks etc is 'flatware'.) No doubt this was a result mainly of supply and demand –

in the larger, richer, burghs more people would have the wherewithal to purchase luxury goods such as silver.

The largest and most important centre of silver making in Scotland was Edinburgh. This was probably due to a concentration of rich and powerful patrons who were drawn to the city as the centre of government, law and the Royal court. They provided a ready market and good living for the numerous silversmiths who eventually set up business in the town. By 1525 (the date of their first minute book) the Goldsmiths were numerous and important enough to have broken away from the other four trades in the Incorporation of Hammermen and set up their own Incorporation, complete with its own deacon and 'serchor' or scrutineer. They were empowered to make sure that all members' wares were

43. Cake basket, made by William Dempster, Edinburgh, 1757-8, for the 2nd Earl of Hopetoun.

marked with the maker's mark, the town mark and, as a sign of approved quality, the deacon's mark. The power of the Edinburgh Incorporation to test the 'finesse' of their members' work was extended by James VI in 1585 to supervise the quality of 'all gold and silver work wrocht and made in ony pairt of this realme'. This was their main public function, controlling the quality of gold and silver used by the craftsmen, and it has continued to the present day. Each item had to be tested or 'assayed', and if it was judged to be up to standard it was stamped, initially with the deacon of the Incorporation's mark, which was changed to the assaymaster's mark in 1681 and then finally to the thistle in 1759, to signify that it was of the correct quality. The other marks that appear on Edinburgh silver are the town mark, a triple-towered castle, and from 1681 a variable annual date letter which enables us to date exactly fully marked pieces. This, of course, was not introduced for the ease of silver historians, but as a means of keeping a check on any malpractice – an early example of consumer protection.

Another facet of the Incorporation's work was to control who entered the craft. Before a goldsmith could become a master – a freeman of the Incorporation – and ply his trade on his own account, he had to serve a seven year apprenticeship to a master followed by three years as a journeyman. He also had to be 'of guid lyf and conversatioun' and had to complete an 'Essay' or test of his skill, judged by two independent assessors. If he complied with all these regulations, and of course paid his entrance fee, he was made a freeman of the Incorporation and allowed to set up a shop of his own, take on

44. Hopetoun Ewer, Basin and Box, made by Thomas Ker, Edinburgh in 1706-7 for Charles Hope, 1st Earl of Hopetoun (1681-1742). They were probably additional pieces for the toilet service made for Lord Hopetoun by the London goldsmith Anthony Nelme in 1691-2, and are engraved with the Earl's coronet and cypher.

45. Selection of 17th and
18th century silver bought
from the collection of the
late Major Ian Shaw of
Tordarroch.
The items shown here are:
(top l-r) plain bullet teapot,
by James Ker, Edinburgh,
1725; cylindrical caster, by
Robert Bruce, Edinburgh,
1708; octagonal caster, by
James Sympson, Edinburgh,
1703; toilet casket, by
Thomas Ker, Edinburgh,
c1705 (made for the
Hopetoun Toilet Service);
plain cylindrical mug, by
William Clerk, Glasgow,
1709. (Middle l-r) orange
strainer, by James Ker,
Edinburgh, c1740; tobacco
box, by Robert Brook,
c1685; covered sugar basin,
by James Ker, Edinburgh,
1724; octagonal horn silver
mounted snuff mull with
Jacobite inscription.
(Front l-r) two-handed wine
taster, by T. Cleghorne,
Edinburgh, c1640;
combined tablespoon and
marrow scoop, by Alex
Kincaid, Edinburgh, 1700;
trefid dessert spoon, by
James Stirling, Glasgow,
1685; porringer, by Harry
Beathune, Edinburgh, 1722;
pincushion, by Robert
Bruce, Edinburgh, c1710.

apprentices and journeymen, and make and sell silver items within the Burgh of Edinburgh.

The 'Lovable trade' flourished in the years after 1700, and Edinburgh craftsmen produced a host of extremely fine and important works of art, as well as a large selection of the more down to earth objects for those of slightly humbler means.

Some of the best examples of their art were bought by members of the landed aristocracy, many of whom over the years built up fine collections. It has been our policy to acquire such collections, either entire or in part, whenever the opportunity arose. Although this can be extremely expensive, it is an ideal way of keeping together items which their contemporary owners considered to be functionally and stylistically linked. The best example of this is the collection of Edinburgh silver accumulated by the first and second Earls of Hopetoun between c1705 and c1760. Over the past ten years we have been able to acquire several items of domestic silver which graced the interior of the original Hopetoun House, designed by Sir William Bruce. These include a very fine, and now scarce, oval bread or cake basket, made by William Dempster 1757-8 (Plate 43). The most important pieces from Hopetoun, however, must be the plain but extremely elegant toilet ewer and basin made by Thomas Ker in 1705-6, for Charles, the first Earl, and engraved with his Earl's coronet and cypher. These were probably additional pieces for the large 17 piece toilet service made by Anthony Nelme of London, in 1691-2. As Scottish toilet services are extremely rare – there is only one complete set known – we were particularly happy to

46. Whisky flask, by D. C. Rait, Glasgow, 1828-9. The base of the flask is detachable and forms a drinking cup.

be able to add to the ewer and basin one of the large rectangular boxes, known as a 'comb-box', from the Hopetoun service. This was also made by Thomas Ker, and was either an addition to or a replacement for the Nelme service (Plate 44). We acquired this box at the sale of another important collection, that of the late Major Ian Shaw of Tordarroch. He built up an extensive collection of 17th and early 18th century silver of which he was a great connoisseur. Most of the pieces in his collection, like that of Hopetoun, were originally commissioned for rich and powerful patrons who wished to give expression to both their social status and their taste by owning objects of value and artistic merit (Plate 45).

Another influential group of patrons for whom the silversmiths made some wonderful pieces was the church. The reason behind their desire for silver was ostensibly at least less worldly, that is to glorify God by celebrating communion with Him from vessels of precious metal. No doubt it was only during this act of worship that the vast majority of ordinary people had

47. Two 'snake-handled' tea urns by William Aytoun, Edinburgh, 1723-4 (left) and John Rollo, Edinburgh, 1736-7. This ovoid form of urn was peculiar to Scotland and like the tea kettle was used to keep water hot, not for holding tea itself. (Lent anonymously.)

any chance of coming into contact with the products of the silversmiths.

Styles of cups and plates used for communion differed according to denomination and also changed over the years. Our earliest piece of communion silver, a cup with a delicate bowl set on a long slender stem, was made by John Mosman of Edinburgh in 1585 and belonged to Rosneath Parish Church (Plate 49). (This was one of two such cups; the other was bought by Huntly House Museum, Edinburgh.) The group of communion vessels which originally belonged to St. Paul's and St. George's Episcopal Church, show just what a variety and range of types were used over an extended period by a single church. The earliest, a flagon by Harry Beathune, dates to 1722, while the latest pieces are cups and patens by G & M Crichton, 1880. It would be hard, however, to match the beauty of the group of four wide mouthed cups with unusual hexagonal stems by Nicol Trotter and Patrick Borthwick which were made for the North West Parish Church, Edinburgh in 1642 and 1643 (Plate 50).

Not all church congregations were wealthy enough to be able to afford to have all, or even some, of their plate made of silver, and had to settle for vessels made from its less glamorous, though no less interesting relation, pewter. The high point in the development of church pewter was the late 18th to mid 19th century, when the increase in the number of rival churches created a large demand for communion plate, and thus provided a healthy market for the wares of the pewterers (Plate 51).

The history of pewter (an alloy of tin and lead) in Scotland starts many centuries

48. Tea kettle with stand and hanging lamp, by William Dempster, Edinburgh, 1735-6 (the lamp by Dougal Ged, Edinburgh, 1735-6). (Lent anonymously.)

49. Communion cup of silver which came from the Parish Church of St Modans, Rosneath. It was made by John Mosman in Edinburgh in 1585, and is our earliest piece of communion silver.

50. Three of a set of four silver and silver gilt communion cups from the North West Parish Church, Edinburgh. The central cup was made by Patrick Borthwick in Edinburgh in 1642, the others by Nicol Trotter in Edinburgh in 1643. They have unusual hexagonal stems on a cushion foot.

before this zenith. The Romans were known to have used it, but the earliest identifiable and datable pieces of Scottish-made pewter do not appear until the late 16th century, when evidence for a settled craft organization also emerges. The pewterers were part of the Hammermen's Incorporation, but unlike the Goldsmiths of Edinburgh, they were never numerous or strong enough to set up their own Incorporation. They were, however, still tightly organized along craft lines, and the Museum has two remarkable 'Touch-plates' which originally belonged to the craft (Plate 52). These pewter plates bear the 'touches', or personal trade marks of Edinburgh pewterers from c1600 to 1760, and we can tell from the existing Hammermen's records who most of these craftsmen were, and so identify any of their wares which they have stamped. The 'Touch-plates', which are the only known examples apart from those of the London Pewterers, were presented to the Museum along with a small oak box or chest with iron mounts and two locks. The tradition that came with the box and plates was that it was the 'charter chest' of the celebrated Border gypsy Johnny Faa. It is far more likely, however, that it was the 'comoun box' of the pewterers into which would be paid entrance fees and fines exacted for non-compliance with the regulations of the craft. Although pewter was never marked with 'assay marks' like silver, there were nevertheless strict laws about the quality of metal to be used by the members of the craft, and it is possible that the maker's 'touch', in Edinburgh at least, was also a sign that he was binding himself to use only good quality pewter.

Two of our most recent acquisitions bear marks of two of the earliest pewterers to appear on the Touch-plates. A rosewater dish by Richard Weir, who became a freeman of the Incorporation of Hammermen in 1597, is one of several known examples which have a central brass and enamel 'boss', which in this case bears the Coat of Arms of James VI and I, marshalled for his use as King of England (1603-1625). These rosewater dishes were possibly used at the dinner table to catch scented water which was poured over the diners' hands from a matching ewer. Our other earliest piece, which was also made to hold liquid, this time beer or wine, is a costrel or 'Pilgrim Bottle' made by Patrick Walker of Edinburgh, who became a freeman in 1607 (Plates 53 and 54). It is exceedingly rare, for although there are a few 17th-century Pilgrim Bottles made of silver this would seem to be the only known Scottish pewter example. It would originally have been fitted with carrying straps or chains which passed through two shoulder loops.

After 1700 the survival rate for pewter becomes much higher and the Museum has tried to build up a wide representative collection of the types of object produced by pewterers. Again, as with silver, this has always been done with reference to historical sources, and we always try to find out as much as possible about the makers. Domestic pewter was made in large quantities from the second half of the 18th century, with measures used in taverns being particularly common. Perhaps the most famous Scottish pewter measure and drinking vessel is the 'Tappit Hen'. It is similar in shape to the cider

51. A selection of communion pewter, from the Martyrs Church, Glasgow. The larger of the two flagons was made by J. Wylie, Glasgow, and the smaller by Graham and Wardrop, Glasgow. The engraved plate is also by J. Wylie of Glasgow.

flagons of Normandy and the name may be derived from the French quart measure 'Topynett'. Measures of all sizes were made in the 'Tappit hen' shape, but the one which the name specifically refers to is the Scots pint or 3 Imperial pints (Plate 58). The use of pewter declined in the later 19th century, being replaced by cheaper and more convenient materials like mass produced china and earthenware.

52. The two Edinburgh 'touch plates' and the Pewterers' 'Common Box'. The plates are stamped with the 'touches' or marks of pewterers who were freemen of the Edinburgh Incorporation of Hammermen between c1600 and 1764. They are seen here inside the Box, which would have held fees and fines paid by the freemen.

53. Detail of the central boss of a pewter rosewater dish which was made between 1603 and 1625 by Richard Weir, an Edinburgh pewterer, whose 'touch' marks the underside.

54. A costrel, or pilgrim bottle of pewter, by Patrick Walker, Edinburgh, c1610. Examples of this type of bottle exist in silver, but otherwise seem to be unknown in pewter.

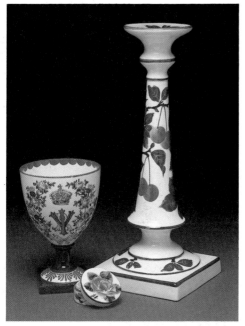

56. A selection of Wemyss ware, showing a typical decoration of boldly painted fruit and flowers. The goblet commemorates the diamond jubilee of Queen Victoria in 1897.

55. Soup plates made by J & M P Bell & Co Ltd, Glasgow, especially for export to the Far East.

57. Coffee pot, by
Alexander Kincaid,
Edinburgh, 1731-2. Coffee
seems to have become
popular in Scotland rather
later than tea. The ivory
insulators in pots like this
prevented the handle
heating up.

58. A 'tappit hen' and a
'mutchkin' of pewter. The
larger tappit hen may have
been made in Edinburgh,
by William Hunter, 18th
century.

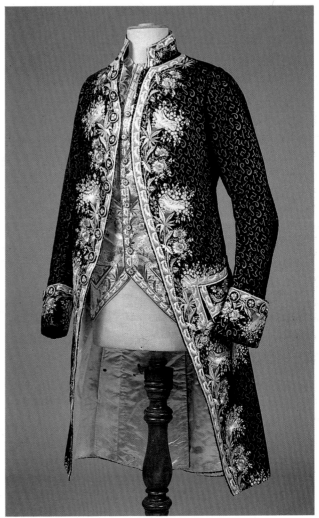

59. Pursuivant's tabard, showing the Royal Arms, Scottish version, first worn at the opening of the General Assembly of the Church of Scotland in 1928.

60. Dalmatic of deep red velvet with decorative central goldwork panel, 19th century. (On loan from St Andrews College, Drygrange, Melrose, per Monsignor Barry.)

61. Purple velvet coat and waistcoat of cream silk, both profusely embroidered with stitched flowers, c1800.

62. Purple and yellow satin and chiffon two-piece day gown by P Maurer, 7 Rue Ambrose Thomas, Paris, c1916.

63. Bondager's costume, the traditional working clothes of female agricultural workers in central and southern Scotland, still in common use until the Second World War.

Costume and Textiles

Of the materials which are the stock-in-trade of museums, textiles are the most frail, the most threatened, the most vulnerable. If they have not survived and cannot now be recovered, we need not necessarily blame ourselves. Museums in past generations did not collect textiles and costume assiduously. They were fragile and techniques of preservation were not highly developed enough to cope with this or with the continuing deterioration which was the inevitable consequence of display. Most museums of material culture or the decorative arts collected textiles, but generally only in the form of costume, uniform or insignia associated with great men or memorable events. The National Museum was ahead of its time in the 19th century in collecting more modest items of dress and adornment which illustrated some of the richness and variety of regional traditions. Thus the Museum acquired knitted socks, caps and other items from Fair Isle in Shetland, a name that has become poverbial in describing traditional knitting patterns, and waistband tape of a type woven on a simple table loom at Balmaclellan in Kirkcudbrightshire. These with bodkins and bone buttons were the slight and disregarded trappings of everyday life.

Later Dr Arthur Mitchell, Secretary of the Society of Antiquaries and benefactor of the Museum, and Gilbert Goudie, historian of his native Orkney and Edinburgh banker, both gave examples of *rivlins* to the Museum. These were light, homemade shoes of untanned leather which had survived in use in Shetland. They were regarded as survivals in a technological and industrial age of the more primitive ways of self-subsistent societies, the survival of the past in the present. Dr Mitchell's efforts for the Museum resulted in the accumulation of what we would now regard as the beginnings of the ethnological collections. If these items are remarkable for their ethnological and regional character, other items are remarkable as interesting oddities. In 1783, the slightly notorious Francis MacNab of MacNab gave the National Museum a deadly sporran; this consisted of a sporran top of brass and steel with four concealed pistols which were fired spontaneously by someone, one presumes not the wearer, trying to open up the purse.

The National Museum's costume collections began to grow considerably and to diversify after the Second World War. The Museum began to develop a strong post-medieval emphasis and in a general increase observable in donations in this period, a significant proportion went to the costume collection. In 1956, the Museum bought a collection of 100 dresses dating from the period 1820 to 1930 and including many accessories which had been collected for the wardrobe of the Wilson Barrett Repertory

64. A table carpet of 'turkey work' from Glamis Castle, Angus. It is a large rectangular carpet, possibly woven in England, with a crest included in the main decorative stripe at one end. This is the monogram of John Lyon, 2nd Earl of Kinghorn, and Margaret Erskine, his wife. They were married about 1618 and we assume that the carpet dates from the first half of the 17th century.

Company. In the following year, the Museum also bought a large collection of 271 articles of mainly women's dress worn by members of a single Border family.

Considerable effort has been made in the last ten years and the costume collections have been established as an important national resource and have been recognised as a very popular part of the public face of the Museum. They have expanded to take account of the technology of textiles from the glories of Scotland's 'linen age' of the 18th century to the exotic productions of modern synthetic fibres. The major part of the new acquisitions had been selected because they were made in Scotland, but this does not mean that we are narrow in our approach. Material from abroad often comes into the collections because it reflects the influences on Scotland through the centuries. Nineteenth and 20th century haute couture garments are popular additions. Clothes designed and made by the top Paris fashion houses for example were appreciated here as elsewhere and are suitable candidates for a national collection.

Articles for the collections are acquired for many reasons, the common attribute being solely that each is recognised as a valid link in our study and enjoyment of the costume and manners of past times. This applies as much to the recent donation of platform shoes and old blue jeans as to the mass of older and less familiar pieces. The word 'costume' seems to suggest a self-conscious approach to dress under the influence of fashion. Another criterion for the selection of dress is function. This may also have been affected by fashion; the vestments of court and

clergy and the colourful uniforms of heraldry have been fixed by historical ceremony (Plates 59 and 60). On the other hand, a national collection is not complete without working clothes. By their nature, they are worn, patched and patched again and are difficult to acquire. They are not without colour and flamboyance and elements of regional uniformity which should be recorded in a national collection. From time to time, pieces of textile are acquired which must be considered as national treasure. The 'Strathmore Carpet' is an example (Plate 64).

This rare example of a turkey work carpet, made in imitation of the prized Oriental floor-coverings of the time, was acquired in 1980 from Glamis Castle in Angus, the house of the Earls of Strathmore. Intended to cover a table rather than a floor, it is rectangular in shape with a red cartouche at one end carrying the monogram 'MEC ILK', the initials of John Lyon, 2nd Earl of Kinghorn, and his wife Margaret Erskine. Comparison of this monogram with that on the plaster ceiling of Glamis' Great Hall, put up in 1620, helps us give it a reasonably certain date, and leads one to believe that the carpet was commissioned as part of the general refurbishment which followed the Earl's marriage in 1618. Its relatively fine condition is probably due to having been stored away when its style fell from vogue in the 18th century from which preservation it has only recently returned to view, and to the practice of covering such costly table-coverings with an outer shroud of leather or similar, unveiling them only for high days and holidays.

Significant as the Strathmore Carpet

65. The Thistle Robes c1687, reputedly those of James Drummond, 4th Earl of Perth. They are a unique example of the uniform specified in James VII's Statute of 1687 which reinstated the Order of the Thistle.
On loan from the Grimsthorpe and Drummond Castle Estate, Perthshire.

66. Two gilded shell collars of stamped metal and a carved and gilded wooden St Andrew badge. These items were purchased with the tabard of Sir John Hooke Campbell and, although the collars have not been authenticated, the St Andrew badge seems likely to be an original and indeed corresponds to those shown in 18th and 19th century portraits of Lords Lyon.

is under the heading of 'textiles', it is equalled in magnificence and historical importance by the recent addition of the 'Thistle Robes' to our holdings of clothing. These splendid garments, on loan from Drummond Castle, Perthshire, are reputed to have belonged to James Drummond, Knight of the Order of the Thistle and 4th Earl of Perth. This illustrious order of chivalry is obscure in origin, a mid 15th century reference mentioning James II's foundation of a brotherhood whose emblem was the thistle. The order fell out of use after the Reformation, probably for its suspected Roman allegiances. James VII reinstated it in 1687 and regulated its dress, stipulating sumptuously, *inter alia,* a 'robe or mantle of green velvet, with tassels of gold and green ... powdered over with the thistle of gold embroidered ... in a field of blue, St Andrew ... bearing before him the cross of martyrdom in silver embroidery'. Alas, a statute of Queen Anne of 1703 reduced this glory to a plain green velvet which, however, suggests that the Robes held in the Museum are of the earlier period, and as such are

67. Heraldic tabard associated with Lord Lyon John Hooke Campbell of Bangeston. The Royal Arms were those in use between 1714-1801.

unique. As well as the mantle, the Robes include a gold-trimmed purple surcoat, sword belt, silver doublet and breeches, stockings and gloves, and (perhaps not original) shirt and neckcloth. The delicate condition of these secondary items unfortunately bars them from display until they can be conserved.

Other articles of ritual and ceremonial clothing held here include a fine collection of heraldic tabards, including one associated with John Hooke Campbell, Lord Lyon 1754-1795, which is accompanied by a carved and heavily gilded wooden badge of St Andrew, the earliest known example of a Scottish herald's badge of office (Plates 66 and 67). Among our many ecclesiastical vestments are now included fine examples of 19th century Episcopalian and Roman Catholic garments, displaying the fine needlework practised in the convents of the time (Plate 68).

These splendours, notable as they are, may well be thought to give a lopsided view of the history they witness. We are however hampered in our desire to give a panoramic view of Scottish society by the fact that the artifacts of everyday life have, by their very mundanity, been little preserved or collected until recent times. Democracy has not long since extended to the world of material culture. Interesting among those working clothes in the National Museum are the 'uglies', black straw-hat or cotton sunbonnets, and other clothes worn by the 'bondagers', the female agricultural outworkers whose survival into the Second World War was the last example of much earlier forms of master-worker relationship in Britain (Plate 63). In this area of the collections, we also have a Land Army outfit of the 1940s.

We intend to expand much further our collection of modern everyday material, hoping that prospective donors will not think only the rare and costly worthy of interest. Let granny's spencer and combinations lie side by side with Victoriana's lace-edged knickers and camisoles.

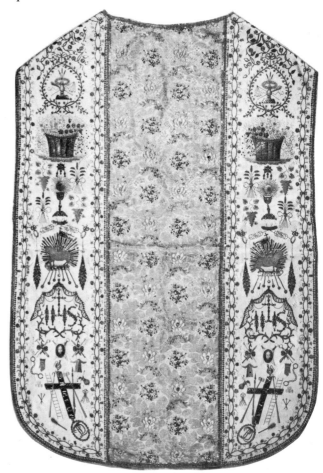

68. Chasuble of white silk, part of a set of vestments embroidered with coloured metallic threads depicting scenes from the Passion and the Agnus Dei, 19th century. (On loan from the R. C. Bishopric, Aberdeen.)

Medals

Interest in medals is considered as a branch of numismatics but it has always ranked as a poor relation beside the interest in and study of coins. Medals are of course stamped pieces of metal similar to coins although often much larger and more highly decorated. Because they are not subject to the same wear as coins in circulation, more artistic energy is expended on them and decoration is executed in higher relief. This apparent lesser status or lower rank of medals in the numismatic order has never discouraged the National Museum. They have formed a distinguished and growing section of the Museum's activities since its foundation and, especially in recent years, medals and tokens have been regularly acquired through purchase and donation.

R. W. Cochran-Patrick MP, the able and influential Secretary of the Society of Antiquaries, helped to secure more favourable terms for the Museum in its search for a new home in the 1880s. He himself was an avid and scholarly collector of medals and recorded information on his subject in published form. In 1949, the Museum bought 135 historical and 19th century prize medals from the R. W. Cochran-Patrick Collection for £780. This may seem small beer in the light of prices paid for corresponding material today but it is even more remarkable that well over half this sum was paid for one superior item, a gold medal commemorating the marriage of James VI to Anne of Denmark in Oslo in 1589. At that time, this one item absorbed the whole of the annual Purchase Grant.

The medal as we recognise it today originated in 15th century Italy, and with the benefit of hindsight we can see that it was one of the most characteristic art forms of the Renaissance. The artists turned for inspiration at first to the coinage of Greece and Rome and the Byzantine Empire and developed their own distinctive styles. Their medals were struck to present a portrait of a leading man or patron, to commemorate his death or to attempt to make him immortal, and then developed to commemorate great events, the consequences of the actions of great men. The reverse face was treated in an increasingly sophisticated way with naturalistic representation, allegory or symbolism. The obverse therefore might be a portrait and reverse an insight into the sitter's personality, and incidentally in most cases highly regarded as portraiture. This was portable portraiture and capable of reproduction like a photograph.

Few early medals of 15th or 16th century date survive in Scotland, if indeed they were ever made. An exception is a medal dated 1491 of William Scheves, James III's busy pluralist Archbiship of St. Andrews. This was probably made in the Low Countries and represents an interest of the humanists of northern Europe. The

69. A silver medal issued after the coronation of Edward VII. The reverse is seen here, but the obverse shows a Lion Rampant flag with the legend 'IN DEFENCE OF THE RIGHTS AND HONOUR OF SCOTLAND'. The medal expresses the same kind of nationalistic sentiments that led to post boxes with the cypher ERII being blown up when our Queen ascended the throne.

70. The obverse of a silver 18th century medal which appears to be a copy of a 17th century original. The suffering lady is thought to be Lady Arabella Stuart, who died in the Tower of London in 1615. The reverse of this medal shows a male and female hand joined – this denotes marriage. The legend round the edge reads 'HOVRT.NOT.THE. [Heart].QVHOIS.IOY.THOV. ART'. The central inscription is 'QVHO.CAN. COMPARE/WITH.ME.IN. GREIF/I.DIE. AND.DAR./ NOCHT.SEIK./RELIEF'.

71. *Opposite (top):* The reverse of a bronze medal commemorating 'The Rebels (ie Jacobites) Repulsed' and showing the British Isles guarded by a fleet and a hand from heaven. The obverse shows a bust of George II.

Opposite: The reverse of a bronze medal dated 1745 issued by the Loyal Association who were opposed to the Jacobite cause. It shows a general reviewing his troops, while the obverse depicts Pallas overthrowing the giants.

Renaissance as it affected the visual arts was late in reaching these Atlantic shores.

The scope of the medallist's art was extended in the 16th century and after the Reformation when propaganda, especially that of leading Protestants, and satire, especially against the Papacy and Catholic monarchies, were added to portraiture. The medal rapidly became a metallic pamphlet, used typically in this period by one nation against another, and recording the triumphs of the one and the humiliations of the other.

Apart therefore from the obvious importance of iconography for succeeding generations, medals constitute an intimate commentary on contemporary events which they were produced to commemorate. Many of course were official and reflect to a greater or lesser extent the artistic standards and fashions of the time. Many were unofficial and were made in vast quantities for the purposes of propaganda or brutal satire, to exploit or to flatter popular sentiment. Often they were made of base metal and the designs crude in the extreme. Sometimes the events which inspired the medals seem of little consequence to us today and yet, judging by the contemporary medal issue, the events themselves caused feelings to run high. The historian must take account of medals as a mirror of history and as a subtle commentary on their times. A series of anti-Jacobite medals in 1745-46 for example betrays the considerable contemporary anxiety for the security of the nation and of the monarchy (Plate 71). In retrospect, this may seem to us to be unrealistic.

Specific local interest in contemporary events may be worthy of comment. Military campaigns in the Low Countries in the closing years of the 18th century may now be considered to be the least known of the many theatres of war of the twenty or more years of European warfare from 1793 to 1815. An expedition to Holland in 1799 under the leadership of Sir Ralph Abercromby was devised to loosen the hold of the French on Channel ports. A medal was struck to commemorate this campaign and it aroused great interest in Scotland. It was spoken of as 'a Scotch expedition' because it was made up exclusively of Scottish troops and commanded by a popular Scottish laird and member of parliament (Plate 74). It also inspired some well known Gaelic songs such as *Tha mi 'n dùil ri bhith tilleadh* and *Blar na h-Olaind.*

For centuries, the medallist's art tended towards a conservatism of stylised presentation in which portraiture was presented on the obverse and an artistic message of symbol or allegory on the reverse. This was the classic form in which medals commemorated great men and events of political significance. The Wyon family of British engravers and medallists worked in an early nineteenth century neo-classical style and entirely in the conventional restrained manner. Medals were also used, like military decorations, as awards of merit. A flood of medals resulted from the expansion of the medal industry when improved minting machinery was introduced during the 'industrial revolution'. The new proliferation of medals was to supply the flood of worthy causes in the 'age of improvement'. The Highland and Agricultural Society of Scotland, for example, founded in 1784, offered large numbers of prizes and very fine medals annually for individual and corporate

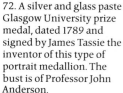

72. A silver and glass paste Glasgow University prize medal, dated 1789 and signed by James Tassie the inventor of this type of portrait medallion. The bust is of Professor John Anderson.

enterprise (Plates 75 and 76).

A later 19th century renaissance in medallic art produced freer styles – always difficult within the small compass of a medal – an assimilation of medals to contemporary Art Nouveau styles of sculpture and

painting, and an escape into plaquette form from a slavish adherence to working in the round. The art movement of late 19th century Europe concentrated on developing links between the applied and decorative arts; medal making united the arts of

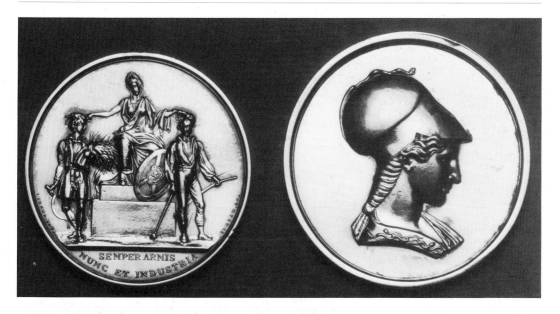

73. *Opposite (top):* A medallion commemorating the marriage of Princess Louise daughter of Queen Victoria and the Marquis of Lorne. The obverse bears the profiles of the couple, and is signed by J. S. Wyon. The reverse shows the shields of the bridal pair, with their mottoes and the date of the marriage, 21st March 1871.

74. *Opposite:* The reverse of a bronze medal of 1799 commemorating the landing of Sir Ralph Abercromby at Helder Point, Holland during the Napoleonic Wars. It shows a crowned obelisk with flags etc, against a view of Helder Point. The obverse bears a bust of Abercromby.

75. The obverses of two medals awarded by The Highland Society of Scotland to Mr Matthew Dunn in 1834 (left) and by the Society of Arts for Scotland to Mr Matthias Dunn, Newcastle on Tyne for his 'Cast Iron Tubbing' 1832 (right).

76. A collection of six silver prize medals, all won by Messrs John Wallace and Sons, agricultural implement makers, between 1862 and 1910. Most are from agricultural societies in the West of Scotland and the Borders, but that on the top right was awarded by 'The United Provinces Exhibition Allahabad'.

77. A bronze medal issued in 1926 and awarded to those who 'gave service' during the National Strike. The obverse depicts a seated figure of Britannia holding an olive branch, with a rose, dragons wing and thistle above and is inscribed 'For Service in National Emergency May 1926'.

metallurgy and metal working on the one hand and painting on the other. Medals were included among the exhibitions of the Vienna Secession movement, demonstrating that these forms were regarded as a suitable medium for those interested in modernist trends in the arts, in *Jugendstil,* and were also a particular passion of artists in Austria,

Czechoslovakia and Hungary. The beholders were mixed in their responses to this art form, either glorying in its sensualities or decrying its decadence. Both Scotland and England copied the modern trends of Continental medallists without developing either an independent school or a distinctive identity of their own.

78. The obverse of a bronze medallion issued for the opening of the Forth Railway Bridge in 1890.

79. A metal plaque commemorating the Scottish Car Rally of 1935, and showing the Wallace Monument, Stirling as well as the badge and motto of the Royal Scottish Automobile Club.

Coins and Banknotes

The Scots have often been accused of worshipping mammon more than most, and the music-hall figure of the tight-fisted, parsimonious miser hoarding every penny is, unfortunately, an instantly recognisable stereotype. Totally fallacious though this is, for there is a world of difference between 'canniness' – a national characteristic that was perhaps originally fostered by the harsh, unyielding nature of Scotland's economy – and meanness, it is true that we have always had a keen interest in our own national currency.

The first truly Scottish coins were 'struck' or minted in the reign of David I (1124-1153). Before this the currency in Scotland had consisted mainly of Anglo-Saxon and English pennies. Even after David began producing his own coins, there was a preponderance of English over Scottish coins in use in Scotland, a situation which continued until the reign of Edward III of England. It should be remembered that right up to the Act of Union, when a unified coinage of Great Britain was introduced, coins from many European countries circulated widely in Scotland, a fact which emphasized Scotland's close economic links particularly with Scandinavia and the Low Countries.

The earliest Scottish coins, mainly pennies, were similar in design to those minted in England. Distinctive features were introduced, however, at an early date such as the shield with the lion rampant on David II's gold noble. This was the first Scottish gold coin and was current at 6s 8d. Saltires or representations of St Andrew's crucifixion were also popular, both first appearing on coins of Robert III. Silver coins with a higher face value than the penny, such as the groat worth fourpence, began to be minted in the later medieval period (Plate 80). The unicorn, one of the supporters of the Royal Arms, was first put on coins of James III, and the thistle on groats of the same king. The 'rider', so called because the king is shown on horseback, was also struck during his reign (Plate 81). These designs were of fine workmanship, and the bust of James on some of his groats is one of the earliest attempts at a true portrait on coins outside Italy.

After the Union of the Crowns of Scotland and England in 1603, the Scottish coinage continued with its own values and often separate designs, although James VI did make some attempt to bring the two coinages closer together (Plate 82). It was only with the Union of the Parliaments in 1707 that the differences were finally abolished and a standardized coinage for Great Britain was introduced.

The Museum has always taken a keen interest in the whole chronological spectrum of the independent Scottish coinage. Over the years an important collection has been built up, and we now

80. Robert III (1390-1406) Dumbarton Groat – Light Coinage. This is a rare example from the Dumbarton mint which was only in production for a short period during Robert III's reign. 'Light Coinage' refers to the change in the weight of silver used in minting which occurred in this period.

have the largest systematic and comprehensive series in any public collection. Our role over the last few years, therefore, has been to identify gaps that exist and to try and fill these and render the series more complete through careful purchase.

It is fortunate that exactly at the time when Scotland lost its distinctive metallic currency, an even more distinctive national paper currency was developed. This became, and has remained until the present day, an integral part of our national economic and social scene. There are several reasons why Scottish banknotes became so popular with the public, for indeed from an early date confidence in them was so high that they were actually preferred to the British coinage that circulated in this country after the Union of 1707. Most of these reasons stem from the very nature of the Scottish banking system itself. From the establishment of the first bank in Scotland, the Bank of Scotland, in 1695, the system developed along joint-stock lines, creating initially a few relatively large public banks with branches all over the country. This generally gave each bank a measure of financial stability (although a few did go to the wall, in only three cases were note holders not paid in full), and also enabled their notes to be circulated and exchanged for goods over a wide area of the country. This 'branch' system was not adopted in England until much later and the growth of innumerable private banks, each with their own notes, caused many problems. It was to curb some of these excesses that the British government introduced the Act in 1826 which prohibited the issue of notes under £5 in face value. The confidence in the

81. James III (1460-1480) Quarter Rider. This gold coin depicting a horse and rider – hence its name – is a very rare example. The Latin legend on the obverse reads 'James, by the Grace of God, King of Scots' while the reverse reads 'Oh Lord, Save thy people'.

82. James VI (1567-1625) Halfcrown. This coin was one of the first issues minted in Scotland after the accession of James VI to the English throne in 1603 and shows the attempt to bring Scottish coins nearer in design to their English counterparts. The Scottish mint mark, a small thistle, can be seen clear'y above the King's head.

83. 'Pull' from original plate (taken c1880) of the Company of Scotland, Trading to Africa and the Indies (the Darien Company). The Company of Scotland was founded by an Act of Parliament in 1695 to establish a Scottish settlement on the Isthmus of Panama which it was hoped would rival England's East India Company. It was also intended to perform a range of banking functions, including note issue and credit facilities of discounting bills and making advances. The ultimate collapse of the Company in 1700, due largely to English hostility, resulted in a deficit of some £232,884.

84. Bank of Scotland £1, dated 2 June 1748 with Option Clause. Following the establishment of the Royal Bank of Scotland in 1727, both the Bank of Scotland and the Royal Bank began collecting large numbers of each others notes and presenting them for payment all at one time which not only caused embarassment but an acute shortage of coinage. The Option Clause attempted to stop this rivalry by allowing the paying bank six months to collect money for payment. Although this action did help to control the worst aspects of this practice, it resulted in the suspension of the fundamental premise of note issue, the ability to 'cash' them at any time. This note is one of only three known to have survived.

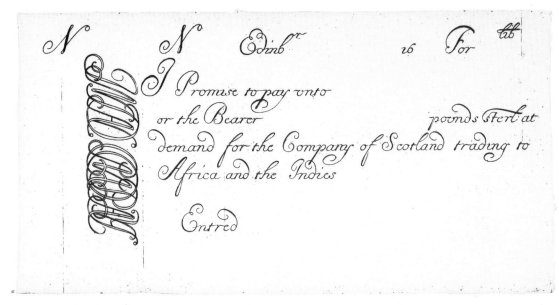

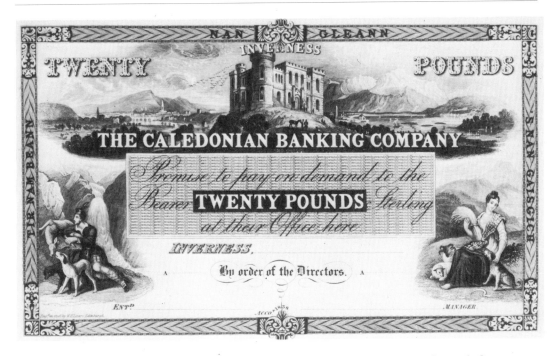

85. Uncirculated £20 proof of the Caledonian Banking Company engraved by W. H. Lizars, Edinburgh. Founded in 1838, the Caledonian Banking Company was eventually absorbed into the Bank of Scotland in 1907. The top vignette shows a view of Inverness with the Castle and the River Ness in the background while the Gaelic inscription reads 'Land of the Mountains, Glens and Heroes'.

strength of the Scottish £1 notes was demonstrated by the huge public outcry that arose when the Government, with a familiar lack of understanding of the often very great differences between the economic and social structures of Scotland and England, tried to introduce this measure north of the Border. It was in part due to the work of that great upholder of Scottish tradition, Sir Walter Scott, who penned the spirited defence of the Scottish notes in his *Letters of Malachi Malagrowther,* that the Government, for once, took heed of the Scottish opinion and allowed the Scottish notes to continue.

Another great strength of the Scottish banking system was that individual banks would cash notes issued by other often rival banks, later returning or 'clearing' them to the issuing bank through the Note Exchanges. This obviously made for a great deal of flexibility in many types of financial transactions. Along with the commendable practice of honouring both known forgeries and notes from banks that had collapsed, this gave the banking system in general, and the paper money in particular, a high degree of public acceptance.

Why are we interested in collecting such apparently mundane, everyday items as banknotes? Are they not, after all simply a convenient means of exchanging goods and services, developed to overcome the problems of the older bartering system? This is undoubtedly true, as it is for all means of currency, and in this way even the most sophisticated banknote is akin to the exotic sea shells used as currency by some Pacific Islanders. However, like the shells, they can also tell us a good deal more about our

86. Leith Banking Company, one guinea, dated 1 September 1825. The Leith Banking Company was founded in 1793 and ceased trading in 1842. The one guinea note shows the arrival of George IV at Leith, where he began his state visit to Scotland in 1822. In the background Leith Custom House which was built in 1811 by Robert Reid can be seen.

nation's history, culture and economic and social development. They should not be seen merely as pieces of paper that can be exchanged for goods supplied, but rather as important and complex historical documents in their own right, one of the sources from which history can be constructed.

What exactly can they tell us? The very existence of notes as a form of currency implicitly reveals a great deal about the general state of economic development. The fact that Scottish banks developed and continued to use these individualistic notes as we have seen speaks volumes about the strength of the banking system. The number and variety of notes is evidence of the numerous banks that were established in Scotland between 1695 and the present. A total of about 70 banks

existed at one time or another during this period, although by 1845 when the Bank Regulation Act was passed this figure was stabilised at 19 'banks of issue'. Through closures and mergers this number was reduced to eight by 1920, and from the 1960s this was further reduced to the three major banking groups we know today.

The dates of certain notes give us clues about the lifespan of their issuing banks and the signatures tell us a little about their personnel. Until c1875 all notes were signed by hand either by an official or by his representative. The huge increase in note circulation in the late 19th century made this impractical, and facsimile printed signatures were introduced.

The designs of the notes have changed markedly over the past three centuries, from simple one sided copperplate

87. Clydesdale Banking Company £1, dated 28 February 1872. The design of this note is a departure from the traditional Scottish style, having an elaborate framework and using the unusual colour combination of green and purple.

script notes to issues that displayed a wealth of detail and colour, which were universally acknowledged as masterpieces of their art. This development not only illustrates the advances being made in attempts to prevent forgery (successfully it seems, for Scottish forgeries were relatively rare – from 1806-25 there were 86 prosecutions in Scotland, compared to England where there were over 1000 during the same period), but also the technical advances of the craft of engraving itself. As we have said, the earliest notes were relatively simple, relying mainly on complicated script for protection against forgery (Plate 84). Up to c1825 they were printed from copper plates. By 1790 the designs had become much more artistic, and the engravers continued to use intricate vignettes showing allegorical figures and local scenes as an anti-forgery device. The introduction of printing from steel plates allowed for much finer detail, and many of the notes, particularly those engraved by W H Lizars, were really works of art (Plate 85). This concentration on detailed scenes continued throughout the 19th century and was incorporated with further developments to combat the increasing danger of forgery. Advances in photography prompted the banks to introduce, c1860, two-colour printing. The use of certain colours, particularly blue or red, made photographic forgery very difficult as they did not reproduce well on the negatives of that period (Plate 89). Throughout the 20th century the banks continued to develop their note designs, keeping well to the fore with technical innovations. Printing on the back of the notes as an additional security measure for example was introduced in

88. British Linen Bank £1, 20 July 1970. This was the last £1 note to be issued by the British Linen Bank before it merged, in 1970, with the Bank of Scotland. It is signed, personally, on the back by the Duke of Hamilton, Governor, Lord Clydesmuir, Chairman and Mr T. Walker, General Manager.

Scotland many years before it appeared in England. The engraved vignettes and scenes themselves can often tell us something about contemporary conditions. Several banks were, for example, extremely proud of the architecture of their main offices and often used these as a motif on their notes. Some used designs based on the theme of commerce and often showed contemporary port and harbour scenes, while others depicted important events of the day (Plate 86).

The Museum has always been aware of the historical importance of Scottish banknotes, and over the past 15 years a determined attempt has been made to ensure that our collection is as complete as possible. As notes were issued on a regular basis by the various banks, it is often possible to know how many types and varieties of note each bank issued, and as these permutations are finite, it is possible to aspire to a comprehensive collection. This is especially true of the period from 1860 to the present, where we have an almost complete series of £1 notes, with only a very few gaps to be filled. Earlier notes, naturally, are more difficult to collect because of their rarity, but again we have a very comprehensive collection. We will continue to identify gaps that exist and try to fill these to give us as complete a picture of this important historical source as possible.

89. Bank of Scotland £1, dated 12 April 1883. The increased incidence of forgery in the 1850s and '60s prompted the Bank of Scotland to introduce two-colour printing. This note was one of the first to use this development. Red was used as the second colour as it was the hardest colour to reproduce photographically, thus making forgery difficult.

90. Commercial Bank of Scotland £1, dated 31 October 1925. Established in 1810, the Commercial Bank of Scotland became one of the largest in Scotland and was renowned for producing notes of great artistic merit.

91. Union Bank of Scotland £1, dated 4 January 1926. Founded in Glasgow in 1830, the Union Bank absorbed many of the older established banks in the South West. It was itself merged with the Bank of Scotland in 1955. This beautifully designed note was one of the forerunners of the reduced size notes which were eventually adopted by most Scottish banks.

92. Royal Bank of Scotland £1, dated 1 April 1953, engraved by W and A K Johnston and G W Bacon Ltd, Edinburgh.

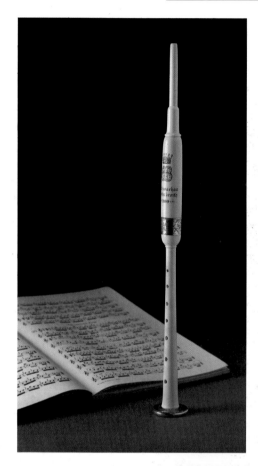

93. Practice chanter of
ivory, silver mounted, by
John and Robert Glen of
Edinburgh, 1880.

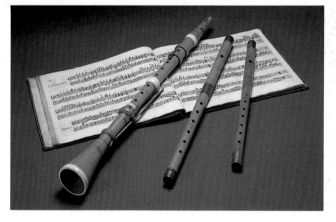

94. Virginal said to have
belonged to Lady Marie
Stewart, Countess of Mar.
This is one of the class of
stringed instruments with a
keyboard in which the
strings are plucked rather
than struck.

95. Clarinet in the key of C
by Longman and Broderip
of London, c1770, boxwood
with ivory mounts and five
brass keys, and two flutes
by Payne and Astor of
London.

Musical instruments are made to be used and in the normal course of events, they deteriorate. The corollary of this is that few musical instruments from past centuries survive. They are of course represented in museum collections in Britain and Europe but by their nature, the old museums collected the rare and the curious rather than the familiar and ordinary, the qualities which also make them significant and historically important.

Possibly the greatest ever exhibition of European musical instruments was held in the South Kensington Museum in 1872. This was of course the Victoria and Albert Museum in its early days. Musical instruments, both by accident and design, found their way before and since into museums of the decorative arts; they were collected because of the quality of their decoration and not necessarily because of their quality as musical instruments. The National Museum had acquired before the influential 1872 Ancient Musical Instruments Exhibition a small selection of instruments including the two famous clarsachs, the Queen Mary and the Lamont Harps, both notable for their decorative finish as well as for historical associations. The first set of bagpipes acquired was the French *musette* in 1871, purchased at the sale of the effects of Henry Benedict, Cardinal York, in Rome and said to have belonged to his brother Prince Charles Edward.

96. Set of bellows bagpipes made by Hugh Robertson of Edinburgh, late 18th century. This is a form of chamber bagpipe which was developed in Scotland, England and Ireland during the 18th century, the descendant of which is the Irish *uillean* pipe of today. This set is unusual for the time in that it has the innovation of two regulators for sounding chords, and the maker's name is marked boldly on it. He was listed in the Edinburgh Directory for 1775 as a Highland pipe maker on Castlehill.

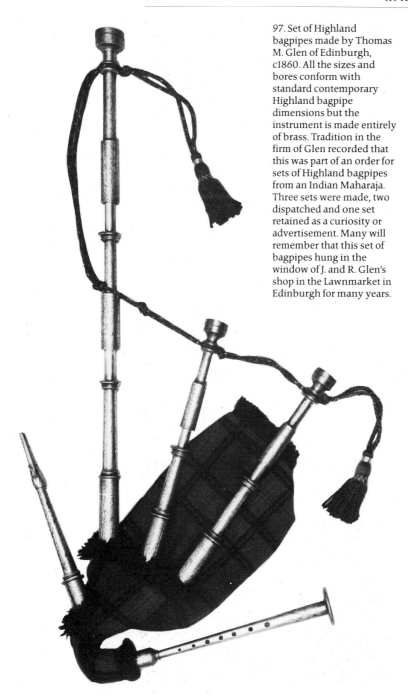

97. Set of Highland bagpipes made by Thomas M. Glen of Edinburgh, c1860. All the sizes and bores conform with standard contemporary Highland bagpipe dimensions but the instrument is made entirely of brass. Tradition in the firm of Glen recorded that this was part of an order for sets of Highland bagpipes from an Indian Maharaja. Three sets were made, two dispatched and one set retained as a curiosity or advertisement. Many will remember that this set of bagpipes hung in the window of J. and R. Glen's shop in the Lawnmarket in Edinburgh for many years.

Although this is a good example of a late 17th or early 18th century instrument, it won its place in the collections because of its impeccable pedigree. The *musette* is a very complicated little instrument and there were not many accomplished performers on it. Prince Charles Edward was almost certainly not one of them, although he may well have acquired this example as a souvenir when he was in Paris.

Museums which include music in their areas of competence or responsibility have to face the question of what constitutes a musical instrument. Some items seem to fit the bill more obviously than others. Keyboard instruments are meticulously constructed according to carefully evolved principles and are acoustically sophisticated. Many woodwind instruments are similarly sophisticated. At the other end of the musical scale, we should perhaps consider that the category of musical instruments should include everything that has been constructed deliberately to make a noise. What else is a drum? Other instruments, of which there are many examples in the National Museum, are whistles and bells, both categories of instrument producing a single sound but undeniably a musical note. Their interpretation depends more on their social and historical context than their musical qualities.

A major cultural movement of our time is the revival of interest in early music. The study of music and lyrics in early sources produced the revival of old playing styles and the searching out, restoration, reconstruction and reproduction of old instruments. A new pressure has been put on European museums by their public, to deliver up the old musical instruments in their collections, to make them available for study or for playing. Museum objects generally have to be only passively appreciated and yet musical instruments cannot be allowed to remain untested and untried. This puts the holding institution in a particular dilemma since the restoration of instruments to playing condition can fundamentally change their character and destroy historical evidence. Handling and use can of course hasten decay. It is the museum's basic responsibility to arrest natural decay. Conservation of a historic musical instrument is the process pertaining to its preservation in its original state or as it has survived into our own day without necessarily any reference to its function past or present. From the museum's standpoint, conservation takes priority.

The conservation and restoration of musical instruments are specialised tasks. It can be said that there are no specialists for this type of work in any museum in Britain. The necessary skills are available in the private sector and have been employed extensively by museums. If possible therefore, early musical instruments should be restored to playing condition and should be played as long as this does not involve the obliteration of original material and historical evidence. As a working principle, restoration need not be obvious but should be detectable.

Music has thrived on patronage, otherwise it would remain at a primitive level. The art and craft of making musical instruments has responded to the same stimulus. The collections of musical instruments in our museums are mainly of the exotic, the results often of excessive patronage. Now we are studying technical

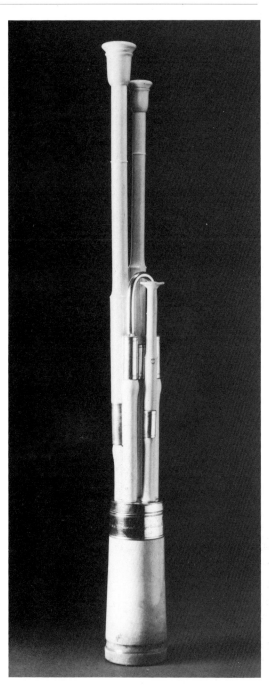

98. Set of presentation drones of ivory, silver mounted, set in a single stock, originally part of a set of bellows blown chamber bagpipes. They were undoubtedly made in Scotland and are of late 18th century date. There was a vogue for the use of ivory in wind instrument making in the 18th century and many sets of ivory small pipes were made. Although they were never tonally successful in comparison with hardwoods, they were usually treasured for their visual qualities.

99. Fife of cocus wood, silver mounted, by Thomas Macbean Glen, North Bank Street, Edinburgh, c1840. The small flute or 'fife' became popular in the 16th century, especially in partnership with the side drum in military and dance music. This succeeded the older tradition of pipe and tabor. The firm of Glen was established in 1827 and survived until 1979. It was perhaps best known for its bagpipe manufacture and repair work although the Glens were very versatile and handled brass, string and woodwind instruments with equal ease and competence. During the 19th century, they made and repaired military band instruments. This fife may have been used in one of the Scottish regiments.

and tonal qualities and collecting instruments for what they can tell us about the history of music. As a national museum in Scotland, we are responsible for describing the musical traditions of our own country and for gathering the scattered remnants from the past of what is still a living tradition.

Clocks

The pursuit of accuracy in determining the time of day has been a major pre-occupation with man throughout his history. In Scotland, the process of technical innovation began with the development of settled urban trading centres. Merchants and craftsmen within these burghs started to demand a more reliable method of regulating their business affairs than was afforded by observation of the sun's passage across the sky. The acquisition by most burghs in the late medieval period of a common clock, or 'toun knock', was therefore a necessary and welcome advance. These early clocks required someone to tend, repair and replace them when they wore out, and from this need the craft of clockmaker developed. The art of these men progressed slowly at first, absorbing techniques and skills from the Continent and England. The pace accelerated, with something of a 'golden age' occurring between c1700 and c1850, heralded by the arrival of the longcase or Grandfather clock.

The Museum's collection of clocks and watches takes account of this development and important examples from every period have been collected. In the past ten years, however, greater emphasis has been placed on building up a representative collection of the work of Scottish clock and watchmakers over the period 1780-1880. The Museum has not concentrated solely on the 'great and grand', the unique examples of high and matchless craftsmanship, although several examples of these categories have also been collected, nor have the fruits of the clockmaker's art been acquired in isolation. Rather we have tried to set the craftsman in his social context. In our collection is represented the everyday work of the large number of clockmakers who earned their living throughout the country supplying good quality, but reasonably priced, timepieces to an increasingly large number of consumers.

We also seek to chronicle the technical developments and innovations that took place in the craft. The verge escapement, for example, was virtually universal in watches made up to the mid 19th century, and a fine example of such a watch made by Ernest Mearns of Banff c1745 shows that provincial craftsmen were perfectly capable of producing first-rate work (Plate 101). By the mid to late 19th century the lever escapement predominated and watches were produced, at first the pocket variety and later on wrist types, that were to remain common until the development of the quartz-powered digital watch of today. George Laing of Edinburgh manufactured a splendid example of a lever escapement watch which he presented to his son, also George, in 1876 as a token of parental pride at his having won a bursary to George Watson's School (Plate 102). This particular watch also illustrates another

100. Longcase clock with mahogany veneer case, dial showing a copy of "The Gentle Shepherd" by David Wilkie, inspired by the poem by Allan Ramsay. By Dilger and Barclay, Glasgow, c1830s.

aspect of the craft. Like many other watchmakers, Laing, although obviously an excellent craftsman, did not make the silver watchcase, but instead bought this in from a London maker. This may well have been for reasons of economy, and it is a phenomenon that was especially evident in the development of painted dial longcase or Grandfather clocks.

The desire of the canny Scots for a solid, reliable yet decorative timepiece was met by this particularly Scottish phenomenon. Such clocks reigned supreme between c1790 and 1870, and many thousands were produced, with virtually every village in Scotland having its own 'clockmaker'. The article they built was a sturdy, reasonably priced, weight-driven eight day striking movement (meaning that it should be wound once a week) with a seconds pendulum. Initially, the cases into which these movements were placed would be made by the local cabinet-maker, although as the 19th century progressed this aspect of the craft became more centralised in the larger burghs such as Edinburgh and Glasgow. The painted dials, which were the distinctive decorative feature of these clocks, were also normally bought in by the clockmaker from firms which specialised in producing them, notably in Edinburgh and Birmingham.

The Museum's collection illustrates not only the technical developments and the geographical differences in case designs, but also the remarkable range of decorative subjects which appear on the dials. Virtually any popular image could be used to decorate the arch of the clock, with scenes from Sir Walter Scott's novels being particularly popular. Illustrations were often

101. Silver double-cased pocket watch, with verge escapement. By Ernest Mearns, Banff, c1745.

102. Silver cased pocket watch, lever escapement. By George Laing, Edinburgh, c1876.

103. Painted dial from a longcase clock by J. Stonier, Glasgow, c1840. The arch scene shows Mary Queen of Scots being serenaded by David Rizzio.

104. Longcase clock with
solid mahogany case, dial
showing the herring fleet
and a sailing ship. By
George Lumsden,
Pittenweem (apprentice to
John Smith) 1814-1849.

105. Longcase clock with inlaid mahogany case, dial showing floral decoration. By Daniel Duff, Paisley. 1830.

copies from paintings by important and well-known artists of the day, as is the case with a clock by Dilger & Barclay of Glasgow which shows a scene derived from David Wilkie's painting inspired by Allan Ramsay's poem 'The Gentle Shepherd' (Plates 100 and 106). Because of the layout of the clock face, the corners had to be filled with illustrations which came in convenient groups of four. A coterie of often extravagantly clad ladies depicting the four seasons was particularly popular, as was a series representing the four countries which made up the United Kingdom. Occasionally more localised themes were used, for example the herring fleets of the East coast were obviously the inspiration for the beautifully executed and designed face on a clock by the accomplished Pittenweem maker George Lumsden (Plate 104).

These highly decorated painted faces should perhaps be seen as a fascinating example of 'folk-art' and no doubt would have had pride of place amongst a household's possessions.

106. Dial of a longcase clock, decorated with a copy of Sir David Wilkie's painting 'The Gentle Shepherd', which was itself inspired by Allan Ramsay's poem of the same name. The corners of the dial are decorated with the Four Seasons represented by four female figures. The clock is by Dilger and Barclay, Glasgow.

107. Mahogany cased
bracket clock with brass
dial, by Thomas Reid,
Edinburgh, c1790.

108. A selection of fashion plates from the collection of the late Adam Dickson. Fashion plates, which first appeared as such in the 1770s, form an invaluable source of reference for the historian and their charm and elegance make them fascinating in their own right.

Symphonie Automnale by George Barbier from the 'Gazette du Bon Ton', 1922.

Rentrons by Pierre Brissand from the 'Gazette du Bon Ton', 1920.

Au Revoir by George Barbier from 'Le Bonheur du Jour', 1924.

109. *Three West Highland Ponies,* c1835. On the left is a bay mare from Barra, one of a breed legendary for its hardiness which died out only a few years ago. In the centre is a grey gelding or *Gocan,* from Mull. On the right is a dun mare from Uist. Like all true Outer Isles ponies, the pure strain from Uist was much smaller than that of the Mainland breeds, but it too is now extinct. Today, the Eriskay pony is the nearest surviving relation of the Barra and South Uist ponies.

Paintings and drawings are particularly vivid fragments of our past and are collected and displayed in art galleries or they might grace the walls of our own homes. Paintings provide a way of looking at the past which is acceptable and intelligible to people. How much they can tell us is a different matter. Generally they are appreciated as works of art and classified as the work of particular artists. We readily conjure up a mental image of 'a Rembrandt' or 'a Titian' or 'a Van Dyck', in which the names have established themselves as strong indicators of style or use of colour.

The Museum, in trying to discover and explain the past, knows that clues are legion and are to be found in a variety of places. Therefore a painting is visual evidence of the past and may be as much a document as a piece of writing. The Museum will not underrate the work of the individual artist or fail to celebrate his particular skill, but it may identify other criteria for adding paintings to the national collections. A painting can provide us with unique graphic evidence of history. Portraits for example of the famous and infamous may represent a real likeness, the artist's predilection or prejudice, or merely a fashionable face. This may be evidence enough but when considering its value, we have to remember that portraiture may be influenced by a range of different inspirations. The sitter may otherwise be unremarkable and only typical of his time, but behind the face we can see clothing and background scenery which may be rare representation of detail which otherwise exists only in the written word. This uniqueness may itself cast doubt on the evidence of a period picture, though undoubtedly, the history of costume and fashion for example would be much the poorer without paintings. The evidence has to be looked at critically.

A recent addition to the collections of the National Museum was the Highland portrait of the Piper to the Laird of Grant. This is one of a remarkable series of portraits painted by the artist Richard Waitt in the early 18th century. He was commissioned by the Grants to paint not only the Laird and his immediate family but also his distant relatives, the cadet families, the tacksmen, local leading men and retainers. Thus while we expect portraits to celebrate the fame, rank, position and wealth of the sitters, Waitt's subjects seem to be of a more modest caste though no doubt formidable folk in their own right. Ian Mor Grant, the Laird's 'Champion', must have been a fiercesome character who seems to glower at us from the canvas and challenge and intimidate all comers. The homely portrait of the Henwife has left us with the perhaps astonishing image of an old harridan absorbed in spooning snuff out of her horn mull.

These two canvasses are not in

Piper
To The Laird of Grant

public ownership, but the other Grant household retainer is. The Piper's name was William Cumming, a fact which we learn from the Laird of Grant's accounts preserved in the Seafield Papers. His figure in the portrait seems rather stiff and formal as he blows and plays his pipes. Behind him are the symbols of status, Castle Freuchie, the Laird's chief domain, and the banner with the coat of Arms of Grant and the strident motto 'Stand Fast'.

A curious detail in the painting is the Piper's instrument. Very few early sets of bagpipes are known to survive in an original state and therefore the evidence for an early 18th century instrument in Waitt's portrait is extremely valuable. But the style and extravagance of the instrument make it seem odd to our eyes and may even cast doubt on the evidence of the painting. It is common even today for bagpipes to be depicted imperfectly in their technical detail and seriously intended pictures to become little more than caricatures. This begs the question as to how far we can accept unique graphic evidence without reserving judgement and searching for more information.

Another detail in the painting is worthy of some consideration and is also one of endless discussion and long-standing controversy. The Clan Grant series was painted between 1714 and 1725 and yet a number of different patterns of tartan is worn by different members of the same clan. The social cohesion, power and influence of family and clanship was no doubt one of the inspirations behind the Grant portraits and yet the sett of the tartan of only two of the subjects shows any close resemblance, that of the Piper and Champion, and none of the subjects wears a tartan with the sett of the modern Grant tartan with its azure stripe.

Another acquisition of the National Museum in the last decade was a large landscape painting commissioned by the Earl of Breadalbane in 1756. The landscape of Scotland was altered beyond recognition by the processes of agricultural improvement. It would be a foreign country to our eyes today, and this aspect of our past can only be reconstructed from the evidence of drawings and paintings and faint traces still visible here and there on the land. The 18th century artist William Sanger was employed to record the hand of contemporary man on the landscape, and this painting and a companion piece of the same subject from the south were intended as realistic representations of the landscape.

The style and intention of these paintings, like the earlier landscape engravings by the 17th century Netherland artist John Slezer for his *Theatrum Scotiae,* make them invaluable evidence for the historian. The artists intended to record the landscape and their perception of their subjects was much more than mere impression. The same eye for detail and faithful intention is evident in some early engravings of social scenes. The Museum has in its collections paintings and engravings of funeral processions which were intended to enshrine the status and

110. *Opposite:* Richard Waitt, *The Laird of Grant's piper,* oil on canvas, 1714. This is one of many portraits by Waitt commissioned by the Grant family of their own family, their kinsmen and, remarkably, their retainers. Several of these people of the Grant clan are shown in tartan although the sett and pattern is different in each case, suggesting to us that the notion of a uniform tartan associated with a particular clan is a modern one.

111. John Sanger, *Taymouth from the north,* oil on canvas, c1755. In the years 1756-57, the English painter, John Sanger was commissioned by Lord Glenorchy, 3rd Earl of Breadalbane, to paint Taymouth, and a companion view from the south of the estate. The gardens, originally designed in 1720 by William Adam had by this time changed considerably, losing much of their formality.

112. Section of a set of four engravings commemorating the funeral ceremony of John Duke of Rothes on 23rd August 1681. They are late 18th century copies by the Edinburgh publisher, Alexander Kincaid, dedicated to the Museum's founder, the Earl of Buchan. The coffin is covered with a pall bearing his ducal coronet. It is carried beneath a canopy which is formed in the shape given to the highest rank in the land. Both canopy and pall are decorated with escutcheons, tears and cyphers.

achievements of noble individuals, to record particular ceremonies but also to provide a conventional pattern and example for the obsequies of others. This was a form of record which had been popular in the medieval period and seems to have survived in Scotland, possibly in connection with the prominence given to feudal and family kinship groups.

Another unique record, possibly formed with patriotic intent, is the processional roll of the 'Riding of the Parliament'. This 17th century 'film' records

the proper ceremonies and dress used at the down-sitting of the Scottish Parliament before the Union, when the members rode in procession with the Officers of State from Holyrood to the Parliament House, bearing with them the regalia or 'Honours of Scotland'. The farther off in time from us and the less evidence which we have available to us, the more easily are we inclined to accept the evidence of such graphic detail although some care has always to be taken in interpreting such processional rolls.

Another series of pictures in the

National Museum's collections can be considered as realistic representations of their subjects. Known as 'Low's animal portraits', they were created between 1833 and about 1850 and hung to the number of a hundred as a teaching collection in the Department of Agriculture in Edinburgh University. The ravages of time and changes of fashion have reduced the collection to a rump of thirty three. These were recently transferred to the National Museum where they are slowly and painstakingly being restored. The second holder of the Chair of

Agriculture in the University, Professor David Low, commissioned a member of the Royal Scottish Academy, William Shiels, to travel the country and record the domesticated breeds of British animals.

An interest in new and improved breeds of animal was one aspect of the agricultural changes of the 18th and 19th centuries. The objects and achievements of the new science of livestock breeding began to be recorded in graphic form from about 1780. The fashion was to preserve the details of outstanding individual animals, and even

113. Sections of a set of three engravings of the ceremonies used at the sitting down of the Scottish parliament, known as the Riding of the Parliament, before the Union. These are late 18th century copies by the Edinburgh publisher, Alexander Kincaid, based on a contemporary drawing, dedicated to the Museum's founder, the Earl of Buchan.

114. *The Fifeshire Breed* – this hardy breed of cattle was thought to be descended from a herd of 'English cows' given as a gift to James IV when he lived at Falkland Palace. However it had all but disappeared by the time this portrait was painted.

to exaggerate features and dimensions to please ambitious patrons. As the 19th century wore on and highly bred beasts became more common, the fashion changed to illustrating breed and general qualities to which animals might conform. Professor Low's intention was not only to record the breed types but also to illustrate the old breeds equally with the new and to give the qualities of the former equal emphasis with the qualities of the latter. This essentially scientific exercise preceded the beginnings of the science of genetics by about half a century. Low knew how important it was to preserve old breed types while building up new breeds, and to avoid breeding out traditional qualities such as hardiness in favour of size of carcase. Not everyone heeded his cautionary message, and vast losses of sheep for example were common in bad winters.

The animal portraits present a unique record of British livestock in the first half of the 19th century. We presume that Shiels' record was a faithful one, purged of the graphic hyperbole of the preceding generation of animal painters. This more or less precise record of animals is contemporary with the beginnings of photography. As photography developed from the 1840s, painting style changed to take account of the competing medium. If Professor Low had had the benefit of technically efficient photography, would he have used this medium for his work? He was certainly keen to publicise his work and some of the paintings were engraved and printed and sold in book form.

Prints are as valuable a source of historical evidence as paintings although the engraver introduces another factor into the process of interpretation. The evidence of course may vary in character from straightforward graphic description to the subtle nuances of contemporary taste – how our forefathers saw or aspired to see themselves. Those interested in the history of dress or fashion will be aware of the proliferation of pictures of dress styles in the 18th century. The National Museum received a bequest of over 1,700 original fashion plates in 1980 from a past Chairman of the Costume Society, the late Mr Adam Dickson. The Adam Dickson Collection amounts to a precise history of fashion in Britain and Europe between the 1770s and the 1920s.

Fashion prints or plates were designed to inform and are generally very detailed, allowing identification of trimmings and accessories and colour combinations, and fortunately for us, they are often dated. Of particular interest too are the occasional traces of Scotland to be found in European high fashion, especially in the 19th century. After the development of an enthusiásm for tartan in Britain, tartan

115. *Orkney and Shetland Breed,* c1835. The ram is one of an old breed from Eynhallow, the ewe is from Rousay, Orkney, and the lamb is crossed with the Cheviot breed.

116. *The Cheviot Sheep.* The Cheviots were natives of the Cheviot Hills and although they were less hardy than the Blackface, another mountain sheep, they grew bigger and gave more wool.

in the form of trimmings as well as Highland dress appeared in the milliners' shops of European capitals. Paisley shawls too appear on the Continent although we know that they were produced in France for example as well as Scotland.

The earliest plates in the collection are from the magazine *Gallerie des Modes et Costumes Francaises,* published in the 1770s in Paris on the eve of the social cataclysm of the French Revolution. The wigs, stays and panniers of the *Ancien Regime* were becoming the simple 'classical' garments and 'natural' hairstyles of the Republic. It was considered important to keep up with these rapidly changing, daring new modes, and in Britain, publications such as 'The Gallery of Fashion' soon followed the French

lead. This was illustrated by the German artist Nicolaus von Heidelhoff and was luxurious, exclusive and aimed at the highest ranks of society. Ackermanns 'Repository of Arts' then gave guidance to early 19th century fashion followers in Britain, when after the Napoleonic Wars the interchange of new trends across the Channel was resumed with enthusiasm. By 1830 good quality magazines were appearing all over Europe and in North America, although they often depended heavily on French originals for their plates.

Wider circulation allowed manufacturers more sophistication. Rather than isolated figures, plates now began to show groups of people in a detailed setting engaged in various activities. Jules David, an

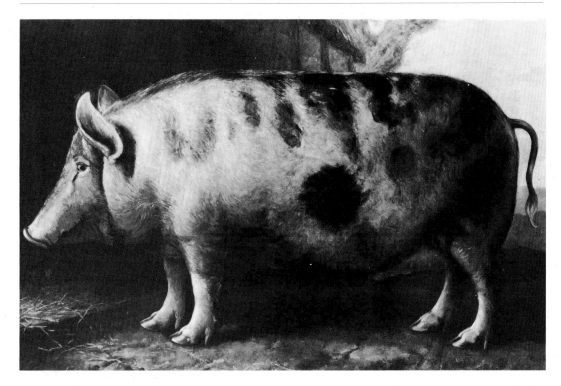

117. *The Berkshire Pig,* an improved breed of pig introduced to Scotland in the early 19th century. By 1884, however, records show that the breed had changed – it had grown smaller and was black although it retained its white feet and tail.

artist who worked for *Le Moniteur de la Mode* from 1843 till his death in 1892, was responsible for many such innovations and his work over almost fifty years exhibits a particular 19th century charm.

During this period most plates still took the form of hand-coloured engravings, and these were produced until the 1890s when colour lithography finally took over. In 1912, however, the hand-coloured plate enjoyed a revival when some of the major Paris couturiers led by Paul Poiret published a de luxe fashion magazine *La Gazette du Bon Ton.* It bears the influence of the oriental splendour of the *Ballets Russes* which first came to Paris in 1908. Brilliant colours and almost unnatural elegance became the hallmarks of the rich and stylish world of early 20th century Paris fashion artists. As these artists abandoned the strictly informative style of their predecessors, contemporary fashion and contemporary fantasy became interchangeable. This is especially true of the albums of hand-coloured illustrations such as 'Falbalas and Fanfreluches' produced by one of the foremost artists of the day, George Barbier. His dreamlike scenes are often highly romantic but are often exotic to the point of barbarism and sensuous well past the point of propriety. They represent 'fashion' illustration in perhaps its most bizarre form.

118. A pair of wrought iron garden gates from Earlshall, Fife, made to Sir Robert Lorimer's design by Thomas Hadden, an Edinburgh blacksmith who collaborated closely with Lorimer.